West, Lunch and Harry's Christmas

also by Steven Berkoff

THE TRIAL and METAMORPHOSIS (Amber Lane Press)
EAST: AGAMEMNON AND THE FALL OF THE HOUSE OF USHER
(John Calder)
DECADENCE and GREEK (John Calder)
GROSS INTRUSION AND OTHER STORIES (John Calder)

West, Lunch and Harry's Christmas

Three Plays

by Steven Berkoff

Introduction by Pete Townshend

GROVE PRESS, INC. / New York

First published in 1985
by Faber and Faber Limited
London, England

First Grove Press Edition 1985
First Printing 1985
ISBN: 0-394-55017-X
Library of Congress Catalog Card Number: 85-14834

First Evergreen Edition 1985
First Printing 1985
ISBN: 0-394-62084-4
Library of Congress Catalog Card Number: 85-14834

Library of Congress Cataloging in Publication Data

Berkoff, Steven.
   West, Lunch and Harry's Christmas: Three plays.

   Contents: West — Lunch — Harry's Christmas.
   I. Title.
PR6052.E588W47   1985   822'.914   85-14834
ISBN 0-394-55017-X
ISBN 0-394-62084-4 (1st Evergreen ed.)

Printed in the United States of America

GROVE PRESS, INC., 196 West Houston Street, New York, N.Y. 10014

1 3 5 4 2

CONTENTS

INTRODUCTION

Pete Townshend

Steven Berkoff has not always been prettily received by British theatre critics. Why the reticence?

Berkoff has strong and committed followings in London, Germany, Israel and Los Angeles. Many young actors use tracts of his plays when reading for auditions. In the élite of Britain's style-conscious achievers he is recognized as one of the new breed, even if he is a war baby.

It isn't easy to commit to Berkoff because he demands all or nothing. When you watch him act, especially in one of his own plays, he is compelling and disturbing. But when you read the lines of his plays away from the atmospheric tension that the theatre provides, the challenge he proposes is directly aimed at all the preconceptions we British hold dearest.

Britain has a fabulous artistic and literary establishment deeply rooted in the past. Even our most daring critics are sensitive to the fact that the average Briton is a conservative soul, quite comfortable with badly played Shakespeare; sometimes disturbed even by the relatively sedate dangers of Pinter and Beckett. Berkoff has often suffered (with great dignity in my opinion) as a result. He is a neoteric spectre who delights in his own paranoia; an actor-manager who hardly seems classifiable using today's criteria. Although he is never an anarchist (for he is really a disciplinarian), Berkoff's work can still seem somehow rootless when experienced against this backdrop of dusty tradition. His plays are written with a rhythmic colloquialism that brings them into line with modern rock music in the realm of current performing art.

Elevation is not the issue. I believe this playwright's measure of friendship is how much torture his audience will endure. In return he wishes to appear willing to bear torture for his art, the audience and thus his friends.

As I walked from the theatre after first seeing *Decadence* in London in 1983 I suddenly realized I had become friends with the manic figure who had directed venom in a jet stream at all the behavioural stereotypes I cherished the most. He apparently despised all the little British eccentricities I treasured. All the detail I adored he seemed readily to abandon. It was as though it was me he wanted – not my vote.

In revealing his inner needs to me through his performance and his play that night, Berkoff obliquely won my vote. This is the paradoxical condition in which he often finds his critics: shaken by his methods, I ultimately respected his courage above all.

The three plays presented here together demonstrate Steven Berkoff's art. *West*, written in 1979 as the companion to *East*, is another clear glimpse of the anguish of city life for the disaffected teenager in search of romance in its highest sense. *Lunch*, written in 1966, confronts the perfectly foolish futility of insular loneliness; a couple enjoy a chance meeting, but never relinquish their pathetic "ideals". As a result they cannot conjoin at any level other than sex and small talk. *Harry's Christmas*, written in 1982, is so revealing of Berkoff's own deeply felt lonely times, and the way they made him aware of his self-obsession and insecurities, that I found it profoundly sad, even knowing his other great strengths.

I hope you are as stirred by these plays as I have been.

▲▲▲

WEST
or
Welcome to Dalston Junction

.

▼▼▼

For Ian, who made this possible

West was first performed at the Donmar Warehouse, Covent Garden, in May 1983. That was its world premiere, although I believe a version was performed in Wagga Wagga, Australia, three years before, in 1980. But they had tampered with the text and even included a scene from *East*, thus disqualifying themselves from being the first to present *West*. *East*, my play about the East End from a young hero's point of view, was the first of a series which, naturally, inspired *West*. The BBC actually commissioned it and then found it not quite dull or ordinary enough for television – much to my delight, as I was then able to stage it at a later date. Limehouse Productions and Ian Albery sponsored its first showing in London, and Limehouse have filmed it for television at the time of writing, so I hope that as *West* played before its thousands, it will soon play before its millions.

West is about courage: the courage to live according to your spirit and not the guidelines laid down for you by others, to be true to yourself, which may involve alienating others, but your truth is worth pursuing since it defines who you are. It shapes, forges and hones you into something that is not vague but clear-cut and definite. Mike's truth is to live for simple principles and to put his courage where his mouth is. He defeats the Hoxton monster and will continue to fight monsters so that others can rest safe in their beds. While the play is an allegory about demons we must defeat, it is also about an area of time and space called London and, specifically, Stamford Hill or Hackney, N16. You wore tailored suits and strutted your gear at the Lyceum, Strand, on Sunday nights. Movements were short, percussive and cool – Ted Heath led the band, Lita Rosa sang and the Kray twins would stand and survey their domain. I never saw them dance. Stamford Hill stood at the crossroads of Tottenham, Dalston and Hoxton and was subject to attacking forays from many directions. Such skirmishes were few, but I remember when, instead of sending a gang each time, Tottenham would send, symbolically, one of their toughest fighters to come and spread terror and challenge our leader. There was one young man from Stamford Hill who somehow elected himself to take on each one, and he did in fact beat them all. He was a frightening cur who actually put his fist through doors for practice. His name was Harry Lee. Mike is not based on a hero but is an amalgam of feelings that I had at the time and my observations of the environment.

S.B.

CHARACTERS

RALPH
MIKE
KEN
SYLV, Mike's bird
LES
SID, Mike's dad
PEARL, Mike's mum
STEVE
MESSENGER

The Hoxton Mob are played by the same actors as Mike's gang
with some subtle changes – i.e. cloth caps and chokers.

West was first performed on 2 May 1983 at the Donmar
Warehouse, London, presented by Omega Stage Ltd. and
Limehouse Productions Ltd. The cast was as follows:

RALPH	Ralph Brown
MIKE	Rory Edwards
KEN	Ken Sharrock
SYLV	Susan Kyd
LES	Bruce Payne
SID	John Joyce
PEARL	Stella Tanner
STEVE	Steve Dixon
MESSENGER	Garry Freer
Director	Steven Berkoff
Designer	Nadine Baylis
Music	Mark Glentworth
Lighting	David Colmer

ACT ONE

Pub sequence. All begin to sing as the lights come up.

RALPH: "My old man . . ."

MIKE: "I'm forever blowing bubbles . . ."

KEN: "Roll out the barrel . . ."

SYLV: "You are my sunshine . . ."

   (LES *and others join sing-song.*)

SID: Time, gentlemen, please. Your glasses . . .

   (*All speak in turn:* "'Night, Sylv", "'Night, all", "Ring me",
   "See ya", *etc., etc.*)

SID: (*To* PEARL) Feel any happier?

PEARL: Well, it makes a change anyway.

   (*They exit from the pub, leaving boys and Sylv. The* GANG
   explodes on to the stage and freezes.)

LES: Breathless, I was aghast when I saw/standing between
   the full moon and the blinking lamplight, this geezer/all
   armed, a certain aim he took/and felled the swarthy git from
   Hoxton with a deft and subtle chop/I never witnessed Mike
   I swear such venom and gross form in leather stacked/his coat
   stitched and embellished with fine lattice work of studs (to
   be more deadly when swung) no other weapon being handy
   like.

MIKE: Armed you say?

RALPH: From top to toe.

STEVE: From head to foot.

MIKE: Then you saw not his face?

KEN: He wore his titfer up.

MIKE: By Christ, would I had been there.

LES: He would have much amazed you.

MIKE: Very like, very like.

LES: His face/his rotten grizzly boat looked like a planet
   that'd been boiled in nuclear wars or struck by meteors/razed
   by hurricanes, criss-crossed by deep canals and rank

defiles/those scars were mute but telling witnesses of battles
fought with weapons/grim with deadly promise/and fought
to bitter ends before the shout of "Hold, hold enough!"

RALPH: No shout of "Hold" was uttered then/not when he
earned those lines/the tailor that did redistribute his face
served his apprenticeship in Smithfields' bloody stalls/had
habit of a thrust and chop to fell a bull and by the likes of
this man's deadly cheeks/was put to death/no waiting time
allowed/they fought until the streets were strewn in blood
and bits of human flesh did gladden many hearts of sewer
rats that night/or so I heard.

MIKE: He must be a right ugly bastard!

KEN: The face doth resemble the asshole of an elephant.

MIKE: A face like that won't launch a thousand ships or pull the
scrubbers to their beds in Edmonton/Gants Hill/or Wal-
tham Cross/so let him have his scars/his medals that he
flaunts to all/to put the shits up any villain that doth take a
fancy to him/for a bout of bundle round the back. That
don't go down with me/you hear/you scum, impressionable
as the tides that lick on any shore and gather up the muck
and floating rubbers from some hectic night that others
have/you who feed upon the blood that others shed/and
wipe the bums of hard-faced villains/living by their very
farts that you gulp down/and think you are so favoured to
be near/that don't go down with me you chorus that
exaggerate some slimy punk/as big in your esteem as you
are small/when seen through normal eyes and not those/
bent with envy/and weighted down with fear/would seem a
normal sort of bloke/a fraction harder than the most at
most/but not a raving Cyclops crossed with Hitler and
Goliath thrown in as well/so pack up all this natter/and
confess the utter wholesome gen (truth) you fancy not my
chances with this Kong?

RON: Of course we doth, my dearest lovely Michael.
(*They walk on the spot.*)

LES: We were only uttering the like of what we saw/
destruction of the King of Hoxton's hardy pack/you know
that gruesome mob/they're hard men Mike/as tough

as hobnail boots/from days and nights of doing bird and
eating porridge within the flinty walls of Pentonville.

KEN: And Brixton.

STEVE: Scholars of notorious hatchet men of Broadmoor/served
their apprenticeship at double time in Parkhurst, Isle of
Wight, 'neath the twins/who taught them ultra-subtle ways
with carving knives.

RALPH: They're brought up hard/since snot-nose kids they never
knew/the softer life/electric blankets when you're snug at night
from pulling scrubbers/from the Locarno Streatham/or the
Ly /that cold walk back to home and hearth/a glass of Tizer in
the fridge and mum's left chicken soup for you to nosh.

STEVE: A bagel warming in the stove.

RALPH: Those dulcet ways doth soften us Hackney lads.

KEN: Sure we'd be good for bang with gang upon a bird/or the
occasional toe to toe with hard-faced Arthur or blond tyke/
from Tottenham/I've seen you fell the best/but those from
Hoxton/they're not human Mike.

LES: They feel no pain/they don't wear coats in winter even.

KEN: Not to spoil their whistles/crush their shoulder pads/they
don't even like pulling talent/lest they disembark their
energy they wish to save/for making love to violence.

MIKE: So that's why all those tarts and slags come running to us
panting/drawers at half-mast when they see a Hackney or a
lad from Stamford Hill.

LES: (*Walking downstage*) Of course/of course/their blokes
just give them clobberings/and pints of crumby bitter/if
they're lucky/and a game of darts/a kicking if they get in
front of Arsenal *v*. Spurs on telly on a Saturday/their day of
rest from hauling bricks around the sites, to harden gnarled
hands to bunch into thick mits or knuckle sandwiches/to
finish off a pleasant evening at the Royal, Tottenham/
they're not for you/I know you're hard my royal Mike – the
King of Stamford Hill/I've seen you put your dukes
through wooden shit-house doors for practice.

RALPH: But those hands were made for better things/like
dealing royal flush and trump beneath the deck.

ALL: Right!

RALPH: Unhooking bras one-handed/whilst the other like a subtle snake seeks other pastures.

ALL: Right!

RALPH: Or making rude and gamey gestures from fast cars at thick-brained yobs from Romford/who in slow and worn-out bangers/can only yelp and scream vile insults lashed in hate/ about the nature of our origin/and flash their rotten teeth/as we slide past in fast Cortinas.

KEN: Birds galore in back/squashed in and squeaking/flapping in their awesome glee at your horsepower man.

LES: So let's forget the bundle/let's scout out what muff walks lonesome streets tonight/and drag them back to forty watts of Eric Clapton or The Queen.

MIKE: Swallow it you mean! And wear a hideous yellow on my back/to strut before a wanton ambling nymph/that's what you see for me/Mike the King of N16/I'll drown more villains than a mermaid could/deceive more slyly than old Shylock would/ and set the murderous Hoxton King to school/can I do this and cannot get his crown/balls, were he Al Capone I'd pluck it down/now listen men of little faith/beneath my gaberdine and/poplin shirts/beneath my Crombie satin-lined with slanting pockets/there beats a heart of steel and will of iron/I'll crack open his skull/with this/I do a thousand press-ups every day and forearm curls/a score of chin-ups on the bar/have made my arms a vice to crush a bear/bench-press 300 pounds/ those triceps aren't just ornaments you feel/500 squats a day with poundage on my back of two grown men/have made my thighs the girth of oaks/and five score pull-ups on an inclined bench have carved a marble sculpture on my gut/feel/go on punch and break your fist on me you snivelly worms/just 'cause my mum fed me with bagels/cream cheese and rich bortsch you think I am a powder puff or soggy stuff thus to be shaped to humping ladies' underwear round retailers or flogging stockings out of suitcases in Oxford Street or doing knowledge on a moped with a dream of owning one fat stinking taxi cab/and sit spine-warped with 30p upon the clock/where to sir? To some ponce who vomits in the back/or has a quick charver . . . no boy/that's not for me.

LES: Our mind's made up.

STEVE: Yeah/let him come/we'll show them what we're made of.

MIKE: That's the way. I see you now/straining like greyhounds
in the slips at Harringay/let's away/arm yourselves my
boys/the heat is on/those that do not fight with us this day
will think themselves accursed/they were not here/get
chains and mallets/choppers and fine steel/we'll give those
evil bastards something to feel/we'll wrap a warning round
their skulls/and they'll not bestride our streets no more/
their ugly mugs scaring the police horses/causing our
pregnant ladies to abort upon their sight and smell/no more
banter/let's go pell-mell to meet in heaven or hand in hand
in hell.

ALL: Smash! Splatter! Punch! Kick! Nut!

(MIKE *starts the words with a physical action appropriate to
each word. The others take it up until it becomes a
choreographic and vocal symbol of an advancing army. This
action reveals a casualty – one of the lads from Mike's gang,*
HARRY, *lies dying.*)

HARRY: Food for w–w–w– . . .

MIKE: Worms, Harry . . . worms . . .

RALPH: Quick, have it away/afore the law doth mark us for
accessory!

(HARRY *dies.*)

(*They race off, running on the spot, then turn upstage and run to
their chairs, leaving Mike's mum and dad,* PEARL *and* SID,
with newspaper each side of the table.)

Mike's mum and dad, SID *and* PEARL, *in their room.*

SID: It says here – pass another cuppa Pearl/that last night
violent street gangs clashed/causing gavolt and misery/six
taken in with wounds/one fatal/caused by they say/rough
Gurkha knives and chains.

PEARL: It's not safe Sid to walk the streets at night/you'll want
some more toast with your eggs?

SID: No, that's fine.

PEARL: A piece more cheese?

SID: Those lousy gits are getting bolder every day it makes you sick/the youth today/you got some Swiss?

PEARL: No, only Cheddar.

SID: That'll do/are all the fish cakes gone?

PEARL: You ate the last one yesterday.

SID: That's all you made!

PEARL: When I make more you leave them.

SID: So – they can't wait in the fridge and give a warm-up underneath the grill.

PEARL: Tomorrow I'll make some more.

SID: Then it's too late/my yen for fish cakes may be gone.

PEARL: That's why you leave them if I make a lot.

SID: 'Cause you don't tell there's some remaining/I always have to ask – you know I like them Pearl! A thousand curses on their guts those swine/the youth today/they don't know what to do but spraunce about.

PEARL: They're spoiled by overpay and telly.

SID: I should smile/filth that comes out streaming from the box and films!

LES: (*As chorus*) Shit, cunt-face, scabby bollocks.

SID: Ugh! You couldn't take like years ago your family out/to queue in one and nines and have a laugh/a sandwich in the bag to munch between the films.

PEARL: You'd always have a laugh.

SID: That's right/you're right/feel safe and cosy/where's little Mike?

PEARL: Bless him!

SID: He's tearing up and down the aisle/laugh! ice-cream from Walls at two pence.

PEARL: Choc ices.

SID: Ice lollies.

PEARL: Vanilla cup.

SID: Chocolate whirl.

PEARL: Bag of peanuts.

SID: Never ate them/stuck in my dentures.

PEARL: I did.

SID: Yeah, you did/all the way through *Road to Bali*, munch, munch.

PEARL: *Road to Singapore.*

SID: *Road to Mandalay.*

PEARL: *Song of the Desert.*

SID: *Wizard of Oz.*

PEARL: *The Red Shoes.*

SID: Beautiful, beautiful, what a picture.

PEARL: *King Kong.*

> (CHORUS *mime end of* King Kong *sequence* – MIKE *on table as Kong and* CHORUS *as planes shooting at him.*)
> Get off the table, Mike, you'll upset your father.

SID: That was a shocker/a cuddle in the back.

PEARL: You never!

SID: Didn't I? Yes I did – and then we'd have a cuppa in Joe Lyons with a pastry/right/they'd make a great cuppa then.

PEARL: They were famous for it then.

SID: The pastries were delicious then.

PEARL: They made the best then.

SID: Rum baba/chocolate éclair.

PEARL: Custard tart.

SID: Lemon meringue.

PEARL: A gossip with our friends all content like don't see them any more.

SID: They don't visit.

PEARL: You don't ring them.

SID: They don't ring me/I should ring them!

PEARL: They should ring us.

SID: That's right – never ask about the kids/never say like years ago/come over Sid and have a cuppa, a game of solo and a natter.

PEARL: You asked them once.

SID: I did/you're right/I won't keep begging them/I should beg them!/What have they done for me? I ask myself. Except to ask a favour.

PEARL: That's all.

SID: Hey Sid – lengthen a sleeve – Norman's grown out of them/take in a seat/you couldn't put a new lining in/could you?

PEARL: There's one in hospital who's still in coma fighting for his life.

SID: They get what they deserve/what they sow/they reap/they
  get as good as they give/I should worry for them?/An
  overstretched health service/and they get a bed at
  once/they should have let them bleed to death.

PEARL: He's still a son to some poor mother.

SID: Unwanted bastard of some brass no doubt/brought up by
  waiting by the pub.

LES: (*As chorus*) When we goin' home, Dad?

SID: Outside the door in all weathers/waiting for his dad and
  mum who's sinking down the pints inside/and now and
  then peek out to see the kids all right/buying them a bag
  of crisps to keep them happy/makes you sick/their little
  noses running/blue knees and shivering/while ma
  does . . .
  (*Chorus sings "Knees Up Mother Brown".*)

SID: . . . "Knees Up Mother Brown" to some joanna that's
  the life they had/witness the clouts their mums have
  suffered at the hands of doltish drunken dad/and emulate
  the like as they turn into them in turn/coming home from
  school all starving with a bit of bread and dripping on
  the table and a note/do not disturb/while mum performs
  with "uncle" up the stairs/breaking in and entry in their
  teens/and then a term or two of Borstal sets them up to
  be the citizens of our fair capital/when once we walked
  down Leicester's famous Square and had/the Corner
  House/a quartet playing/lunch at half a crown.

PEARL: Those were the days.

SID: The Salad Bowl.

PEARL: Mixed Grill.

SID: The Guinea and Piggy.

PEARL: All you could eat for a guinea/imagine.

SID: I kept going back for more/remember? He couldn't
  believe his eyes.

MIKE: (*As chorus*) You back again?

SID: Five times he saw me/fill it up I said/the plate was up to
  here/I wolfed it down though/went back again/all you could
  eat that's what it said/there's nothing they could do.

PEARL: They closed it down that's what they did.

SID: Not on account of me! 'Cause hard-faced layabouts would
    lay about at night/and put the wind up decent folks.
CHORUS: Hey Jimmy, gie's a drink!
SID: That's why they closed it mate/the West End's now a karzi.
    (*Chorus mimes vomiting.*)
SID: Now you dare not walk the streets at night/lest some
    unsavoury mugger/some huge schwartzer maybe/takes an
    eye to you.
CHORUS: What you lookin' at?
SID: Or drug-crazed hippy dying for a fix decides to stick a
    bayonet in your guts for half a dollar.
PEARL: I'm nervous going to bingo even and that's only down
    the road.
SID: Nobody phoned, eh?
PEARL: No, shall I ring Rosie/ask them round for tea on
    Sunday.
SID: We should ring them! When do they ring us?
PEARL: You're right Sid/you're quite right.
SID: Be independent/don't be proud to be a little independent.
PEARL: When you're right, you're right/maybe she rang and we
    were out.
SID: So did she try again?/You'll make fish cakes tomorrow.
PEARL: Yeah, I'll make a load/only who will eat them?
SID: I'll eat them/don't worry/I'll eat them!

Hospital. A bed. The face of HARRY, *dying, quite still. The table is
the bed.*
LES: It was our fault that little Harry fell/his memory
    shall be honoured for all time/stabbed in the field by
    coward's hand.
RALPH: This will not go unanswered/he shall be avenged.
KEN: Eye for an eye/tooth for tooth.
LES: We had them on the run/they fled beneath our
    might/but one fell rat draws out a knife to leave his mark
    behind.
KEN: The canker of the nether world/they are a plague that we
    must crush/or else they'll grow/contaminate by touch.
RALPH: What's the answer/blood for blood?

(*Music stops.*)

MIKE: You must strike at the top/cut off the head and then the
body's dead/confusion then will spread about/then we mop
up/to get into the hornets' nest and kill the king/not battle
in the streets/but plan concerted armed attack/he's hard you
say/invincible to some/but he's only a human like us all/with
feeling senses/if you kick him does he not hurt/if you stab
him will he not bleed?

LES: To go into the lions' den is begging for it/they'll smell
us at a mile/they'll see our homespun spotless faces/not
scabby/lined with tracks like Clapham Junction/they'll sus
us out before we're even near and wipe us off the streets.

MIKE: A little camouflage is what we need/divest yourselves of
your smooth gear/and imitate the clobber of that mob/
cheese-cutters and football boots/a choker round our neck
in white/a black shirt here and there/and dirty up.

RON: That's great/I'll drink to that/let's make a ding-dong at
Dave's pad to celebrate this plan/you're all invited/bring
some booze the birds laid on/some slags he pulled from
Dalston double-hot in keenness/and mad to make acquaint-
ance of you Mike.

KEN: Yeah I double fancy that/right on mate/I'll change my
knickers/let's get the booze.

MIKE: Do not forget what we have said tonight/don't let this
booze-up blunt our dreaded purpose.

LES: Nay!/We will speak further on it/oh come on Mike/let's
mix our grief with some small joy/to celebrate destruction of
the beast/we'll make our plans tonight and fix the day!

MIKE: OK, at the Duke's Oak we meet/that's on the way.
(*Boys' pub talk: "Five pints, Bert." "Straight glasses, if you
please."*)

*Mike's bird, SYLV, in her room. Boys and family act as simul-
taneous background from their areas: pub at top; PEARL and SID in
centre; SYLV at bottom.*

SYLV: It was November/the last dead leaves of autumn/were
falling off the perch/the day was cold as ice/flawless sky
mind you/like it was washed in Daz/the pigeons picking at

the hardened chunks of dogshit/it's silent, like a Sunday is
round here/and I went down the road to get the *Sunday
Mirror*/and some fags/the OAPs were snivelling in their
scarves they wrap around their sunken sucked-in cheeks/as
they bought cat food for their sole companions/their chat
was shrill with "Hallo Dot and how's your chest" and
"Innit parky, half a gallon of paraffin"/and back they went
swaddled in veins and rheumatism to their grim/stove on
the landing/room/cold water and a pic of dad/when he was
fighting for his king for three and six a week/a postcard on
the mantelpiece from daughter seen just once a year/at
Xmas maybe/or a death/it's funny that I sit in now and wait
for him to ring/he said he would today.

MIKE: Go on, Les. Put something on the jukebox.

LES: What d'ya want – Rosemary Clooney?

PEARL: Must we watch telly all the time? Let's play cards.

SYLV: Mike usually decides to come over/that's so nice/we sit in
   watching some old flic on telly/or playing Perry Como or
   some Brahms particularly he likes the Fifth by Beethoven/it
   gets him all worked up he says though/I like dancing really
   to some Latin/we jump around a bit and shake a leg/we'll
   have a fag or two/or smoke a joint/maybe a benny just
   before our lunch/I'll warm a frozen curry from the
   store/maybe Fray Bentos/though Chinese from the takeaway
   is nice/some nice chop suey and some chips/that's good, I
   fancy that and he don't half love it as well/I'll get that in a
   minute and what else/I think that's all . . . oh come on
   Mike and bloody phone you bloomin' bore.

MIKE: Not too much, Ken.

KEN: Five more pints, Bert.

SID: Oh my ulcer! Pulverize a couple of pills, Pearl!

SYLV: Suppose I get it all and he don't come/I'll keep it for
   tomorrow/I'll do that he ain't half nice – really he is/he has
   his funny ways/I mean who don't/and sometimes I could
   strangle him/but when he looks at me with those hurt eyes/I
   just want then to mother him/he's really handsome like a
   movie star/but rugged like not poofy but a cross between
   Paul Newman and Brando/with little hints of Redford and a

touch of Cary Grant or maybe Boris Karloff/he don't half make me laugh sometimes/we'd laugh so much they'd knock back on our walls/those from next door – that woman who is always sick and lives with her mad son who never works/oh come on Mike.

MIKE: So go on, ask me: do I care?

BOYS: Do you care?

PEARL: Dorothy said she might pop in tonight.

SID: I'm out!

SYLV: I can't remember did I take the pill today or not/oh piss I lost my little card/oh never mind/but then suppose he wants to then what do I do/oh never mind one day won't hurt or will it/no I shouldn't think it would/or would it/rules are rules and if you break them then you take the risk – men! Much they care – but then they're not supposed to – really/they never do.

STEVE: Seein' Sylv tonight?

MIKE: Nah. Givin' her the elbow.

LES: How about Ange?

PEARL: Turn it off, for Christ's sake.

SID: It's the weather forecast.

SYLV: I can't go through all that again/no God forbid/I just can't go back to that vile place/and let them in to murder part of me again/like opening your doors to killers in white coats and saying/it's in there – you will be quick/it won't hurt it – will it?/No! No! Not again/oh come on Mike I'm getting bored hanging around – it's Sunday – come on ring you sod.

RALPH: So I said, pal, do I look like a tin of dog food?

SID: Go to bed.

(SYLV *takes fag out – looks in mirror. Lifts her skirt – suspender belt, garters.*)

SYLV: Couldn't resist it really – he likes that – it's cheeky/I feel funny in the street/funny and nice at once/to know what's underneath/and no one else suspects/how could they/I'll give him a surprise/that's if he wants surprising that is/don't know lately if it's getting/well . . ./better or worse/can never tell with him/or maybe he's getting something else to play with/bastard bet he has/oh if he dares! Maybe that's it/it's

wearing out/it's not the armed assault like once it was/then
he'd come at me like I was the last bird in the world/he said
he loved me then/after the op he turned all funny for a
while/chop suey or a curry – maybe a plate of spags/oh ring
you git I can't stay in all day and wait and wait.

LES: Here's to a smooth and slick funeral!

PEARL: It's just a blank screen, Sid!

SYLV: I fancy going up West/I'll treat him to a film and we'll sit
in a nice wine bar/I'd like to meet some people/for a
change/just watch them even/sick of staying in/oh come on,
ring me, please ring! Please ring – please ring.

RALPH: Do you all know the way to Dave's? First right, first
left.

PEARL: I'm going to bed.

The gang at a table – harsh white light.

MIKE: A score of broken bones and busted schnozzles was the
price we paid by being unprepared.

RALPH: By being unprepared we was caught out with knickers
well and truly down.

STEVE: They came back for revenge last night/for the almighty
pasting that they took as if poor Harry's precious life was
not enough to slake the creature's thirst.

LES: The brute and monstrous thing rose from its lair into
the thick sulphurous night/while we were snoring gorged
appetites like swinish pigs/well bloated and obscene from
"evening in" with favoured bints/their perfumed limbs
enwrapped us like some marble seraphims/the sweetness of
their breath, so honeydewed mellifluous with tinkling
flute-like voices/beguiled us with soft porn suggestions/in
the dales and valleys of our ears/and we unpeeled them like
it was a ripened plum or mango – satsuma or sweet pear.
But they were poisoned fruit/within they carried
venom/between their loins a praying mantis/sucking us to
our death in lust-filled swoons/for they had plans/the birds
we pulled last night were fronted for attack/were set up to
assuage us in our guard by rendering unarmed our finest
men/attacking us where we are vulnerable/our sensual

centres/famed to all the world/those cornucopias of
passion/our Achilles' heel/our Samson's hair/where flock the
sirens of the Western world/to feed and drink in our rich
pastures/welcoming them all/turning none from our
door/those starved within the barren regions/of Dalston,
Enfield and Wood Green/who flocked to Stamford Hill.

MIKE: Oh horror! Horror! Horror!

RALPH: We planned too late our deed/we should have struck
when he was bloated in his bed as he found us/instead of
deeds/we fell to carousing as if to celebrate the victory
before it's won.

MIKE: Oh you my sinews bear me stiffly up!

RALPH: We were a cinch/lucky for you that you were out/the
stroke of fate that did decide by tossing coins/you were the
chosen one to buy the shish kebab from takeaway/or else
you may have suffered that like fate/that marched so
painfully upon our undefended loins.

MIKE: My fate cries out and makes each petty artery in this
body as hardy as the hardest villain's nerve/I'll tear him all
to pieces!

ALL: You shall not go.

MIKE: Unhand me/by heaven I'll make a corpse of him that lets
me/I say away! I warned you/what did I say! You were
seduced by snatch/your watchman fast asleep/his potion
drugged no doubt/allowed yourselves to be disarmed and
floating in the ether of vile lust/so's not to hear the hobnail
boots they always wear with toes steelcapped in dread/you
mugs/what are you/with friends like you I don't need
enemies/you were outshrewded by the Hoxton fiends/who's
celebrating now, no doubt in City Arms/carousing with his
chinas of/how easy it was after all/and laughing with loud
chortles/while the blast of shame sits on our brows like the
ill mark of Cain/now who comes here?

(A MESSENGER approaches.)

MESSENGER: I come unarmed from Hoxton's mighty King/to
give a message to him that calls himself/the Prince of
Darkness/the King of Stamford Hill or just plain Shtip-it-in
Mike.

MIKE: I'm known by many names but those will do/say what
   your business is and blow/you emissary from the
   underworld where sunshine never comes and days are
   choked in hell's polluted smoke/say what brings you here to
   gloat upon your master's cowardice and treachery.

MESSENGER: Cut out the patter man and cock an ear to what
   my honoured master hath to spout.

KEN: You dare to speak like that you pint of gnat's piss.

MIKE: Let him go.

MESSENGER: And wisely said/that you may learn a thing or
   three/I see you are the guvnor/so here's the spiel/to cut all
   these wars which doth confuse the citizens of our
   strife-warm manor/to halt the battles in the Royal
   Tottenham which hath us banned from dancing with our
   chicks/and making parley with our mates/to cease the clash
   of skull and iron in our streets which doth excite old johnny
   law to exercise his tool on us/and bring the black marias out
   like wailing banshees/round our council flats/in other words
   a one to one – just you and he – step round the back – by
   some remote deserted track/the Hackney marshes/or
   designate a place that you prefer/I'll pass the message on.

MIKE: The marshes suits me well/tell him I'll come.

MESSENGER: Upon the stroke of twelve/one week from now.

MIKE: I shall be there.

   (MESSENGER *exits*.)

LES: I do not doubt some foul play.

MIKE: A one to one/it's what I've always dreamed of.

KEN: What if he should lure you into some forbidden trap and
   there . . . phut!

MIKE: What should I fear/when I now sense a giant strolling in
   my veins/now I could slay whole armies all alone/a one to
   one/I wish there were a hundred just like he/a week from
   now/till then sit still my soul/for Hackney marshes will
   become the bloody sea.

   (*They trot off in quasi-military fashion. Exeunt. Fanfare.*)

SID *and* PEARL *in their room. They speak but not to each other.*

SID: Soho's not what it's cut out to be.

PEARL: I get bored watching telly every night.

SID: There was a time when it was fun to walk the streets in
summer/birds out on the game/all legs/then to stand
about/flaunt themselves for all to see/you knew what you
were getting/not that I got/but for a laugh you'd ask how
much/and go up to the next/it passed the time.

PEARL: Sometimes I'd like to pack my bags and leave him to it/just
run out and go/I don't care where/just up and off/and never see
his face again/it's too late now/I should have done it long ago.

SID: Where did it go wrong I ask myself/she never had to do a
stroke of work/I brought home all my wages every week/not
all mind you but they never went short.

PEARL: He's not taken me out in years/not once in years like/
come on Pearl let's drive to Brighton for the day . . .
(*Tableau as* BOYS *and* SYLV *join in and re-create the scene.*)
. . . it's sunny out/we'll pack a lunch and take the kids I
used to like it years ago/the pier and stroll along the prom/
sit on the beach and watch Michael throw pebbles in the
sea/and then a game of housey housey it's called bingo
now/we won a silver-plated teapot . . . (*Scene disappears.*)
. . . where has it gone I wonder?

SID: The others all made profits from the war/I was an honest
joe/I could have made a fortune/with a little simple
graft/black market was the rage.

PEARL: But for the kids/I'd have slipped out long ago/but when
you're tied it's difficult/how could I leave them/or support
them in a furnished room/it's just for them I live – it's for
the twinkle in my baby's eye that I can soldier on/not that
he's an angel but he's all I got/and she's as good as gold.

SID: They're ingrates that's the truth/give us a quid or two dad/
or a tenner/or a pony maybe/pay you back? No
never/sponge on my old bones till I drop dead/I'd like for
once to see him looking smart/a decent hair cut/a well-cut
suit instead of that costume he wears/the layabout.

PEARL: I look at him and think what have I got but habit and
some sleeping pills/to send us to oblivion at night or ease the
pain of our arthritic bones/to soften his loud snores and give
an hour or two of sweet forgetfulness/one day I'll take the lot.

SID: Harry's boy did well/matriculated and all that/then
college/then degree in this and that/a clever lad/stopped in
most every night to fill his cop with knowledge/he's no
schmuck/and the skill to stand up in a court and be a man/
defending companies in the quagmire of business laws/what
a man is Harry's boy/his mum and dad he bought a home in
Chingford with a garden and drives a Ford Estate/what did
my son achieve for us – gavolt and anguish fear for every
knocking on the door/in case some johnny law should say
we're looking for . . .

PEARL: Some wives have husbands who's a joy/so proud they
entertain/and lay a table for their friends on Sunday night . . .
(*Party tableau. "Hello, lovely to see you", etc.*)
. . . a drink of port/and tell some jokes/maybe a game of
pontoon/silver laid/and lumps of children everywhere/
daughters and sons/grandchildren too/to fuss over/their
grannies take them out/their fathers proud and braying the
achievements in the world of their most honoured kids/they
don't invite us any more . . .

LES: 'Bye, Aunty Pearl.

SYLV: Lovely meringues, Pearl.

MIKE: Ring you.

PEARL: . . . and I can't go alone/he says he's too tired to go
out/and/what have they done for him he says/you've only
got to entertain them back/so we sit in and watch the telly.

SID: I showed him how to earn an honest buck/I only told him/
get out now and graft/did I do something wrong/to turn him
to a villain/lousy sponger/low-life that he is/who comes
home when he does with busted teeth and broken bones
and God knows where he's been or what he's done/if he
stayed in and copped a book or two or got a decent job
when he was young instead of dancing out all night with
stinking whores no doubt/the filth he mixes with is rife in
bad contagion/if he had worked he's got some brain/he
could have been a manager at least of Cecil Gee's/or maybe
an accountant/Tucker that's a job! For that you need a
noodle in your bonce/faa! A pervert for a son/to tell the
truth no blood of mine but hers.

PEARL: He set him no example if he's bad.

SID: From her and all her spoiling he's no good.

PEARL: When did he get a father's love/I ask myself.

SID: She always favoured him/right from the moment he was born.

PEARL: He never took an interest in him the way a father
should/to show him what it is that he should know.

SID: What time does *Hawaii Five-O* come on?

PEARL: Eight o'clock.

SID: Turn it on, will you love?

GROUP: I fancy going down the Royal/I double fancy that/the
Mecca is my temple of fate/who shall I pull/who shall I
meet, will she be wrapped up like an Xmas treat/the fireball
is turning, the music starts/your eyes survey the crumpet/
and you say, do you wanna dance, do you wanna dance?

BOYS: Do ya wanna dance?
(MIKE *takes* SYLV *on to the floor, just the two of them. The*
BOYS *are upstage, acting as a chorus line with invisible partners.*)

MIKE: Do you wanna dance/we slid on to the floor like two seals
in a pool/wearing an ashen look about her face/smelling like
a perfume counter at Boots/she had that look about her/like
I couldn't care if you dropped dead look/her eyes scanning
other talent/searching out the form/of course we do not get
too close/just enough to give a hint of things to come/a lasso
of lust waves encircles her.

SYLV: He . . . he looks like any other/with easy grin/street-corner
patter/so we dance a bit and then he asks me.

MIKE: Do you fancy a drink?

SYLV: With him/as if he bought me/for a dance/whereas I stand
or sit with or without mates/watching lines of faceless
trousers stomping up and down.

MIKE: She looks nice.

SYLV: He looks OK/nice eyes/love crumbled grey/and smoking
already for me/he says he don't half fancy taking me home/
back to my gaff/an arm squeezed.

MIKE: Fancy her/not much I don't half.

SYLV: Yeah another gin and it/lipstick smudged/I'll do my hair/
excuse me.

ALL: Thanks luv/that was nice/enjoyed that/fancy a drink/where
d'ya live? – oh!

MIKE: I got to the karzi/full of geezers doing their barnets and
who has who.

STEVE: I'll take the ugly one.

LES: Yeah all right!

KEN: What a cracker.

RALPH: I didn't get nothin'!

MIKE: And all that/I take the future of England in my hand and
ponder her body which seems to me as if a shoal of silvery
fish were gathered in a net/and wiggling and slithery with
her silken skin encasing her incredible form.

LES: Mind the strides, pal.

MIKE: Whilst I read what Kilroy has been up to/so after much
chat and I don't know/the night was wearing thin and I
became afeared that unless she yielded to my heart-felt
quest/to take her home that is/these chicks/these panoplies
of exquisite and sensual delights/would be booked up by
other snatch-bandits staking out their prey for the night and
if at 12 o'clock I walk home on my tod sloan I would be
well and truly choked.

SYLV: Not tonight, let it not be tonight.

MIKE: All right just to the door/unless . . .

SYLV: No, I said not tonight.

MIKE: Why wait/what makes it better if you wait/it's cold out
here/let's go inside/her make-up's cracked beneath the
light/our breath steams and snorts.

SYLV: He should wait/else I'm just another receptacle to stomp
out his butt/he pushes himself against me like I was for him
a sanctuary that he was struggling to get into.

MIKE: Like I was pursued by wolves/and she took my breath
away.

SYLV: And he asked me out next day/and from then on all I
wanted was to be a sacrifice/like an offering/I can't help it/
how often can you feel that/and that's how I felt/and he felt
good to me all the time/and often/not like the others but
someone wanting someone like me/and now why won't the
bastard ring?

The lads jump in attacking stance.

MIKE: Like stepping round the back was what was expected of you/like a clobbering now and then/was mixed up with pulling birds round there for stand-up charvers/like that very spot where now you gaily spray your spunk/was where two nights ago you splattered blood/'gainst that very wall/ you pulled in passageways/in doorways/in any nook and cranny so you'd only exercise your passion in the dark and private/with a bird/or bloke for violence or love/or be in love with violence/so when two tearaways decide to bundle/to inflict some GBH upon each other's form/they might be making love/and seeking out the soft parts to inflict upon them some unsightly woe/and finish off the night in blissful satisfaction/of adrenalin well pumped and flushy bleeding faces/all lit up with joy/and many hand thumps on the back.

STEVE: You did all right, mate.

LES: Yes?/you din half give him one/boot in like –

RALPH: Kicked the shit out of –

KEN: I liked the bit when –

STEVE: Well and truly.

LES: Handsome/ta da!

STEVE: See ya!

LES: Look after –

KEN: See you, plater.

RALPH: All the brest.

KEN: So he decided that it had to be and so prepared himself for the onslaught/toe to toe and nose to nose/the weapons chosen/and us chinas to be there in case the others thrust their grubby maulers in.

Gym. MIKE *training with weights/during this last speech/pushing weights in conjunction with music/muscles bulging/veins swelling/sweat pouring off in shower/the mates continuing their foreboding text.*

RALPH: I've seen the brutish thing he has to slay fancy his chances/I don't know/I hate to tell my mucker/my best

mate/that I might carry in my heart/a little doubt/so I'll
keep schtumm/and render him my total confidence in this
night's caper.

LES: The other bloke annihilated last week/was in a coma
for some days/between the sheets he bled/and put tubes in
both his ears/to see if he was leaking red from broken
tissues/or the brain/that's what they do/and shoved up little
things into his nose in case he haemorrhaged and formed
a clot and shaved his head and searched his skull in case
his mind was cracked/or broken/but he recovered to tell
the tale.

STEVE: And was it worth it after all/I'd be rather all tucked up
and wrapped around a softer creature/dragging kisses up
from the deep/than face a bunch of fives well clenched/I do
not fancy kissing that at all.

MIKE: But who can undo what has now been done/or wipe the
writing off from on the wall/what has to be will be.

*Walking home after the gym, bag over shoulder. Music. Each one
follows the other and takes over the walk.*

RALPH: Walking home alone beneath the stars/up Amhurst
Road/to Manor House/and down to Finsbury Park/where
little ducks sit quietly at night/like toys in a lake of glass/to
lonely back streets after/nights of rock and roll at the
Rainbow/or James Bond giving her one at the
Essoldo/Maybe a binge at some vomity local/going home in
pairs/to make it in the back of steamed-up Minis/I could not
help but wonder on this night of all the talent getting well
and truly laid/and all the grinding going on/and how many
and how much/and all the wails and screaming going on
right at this moment/could almost in the silent aching
streets/hear across the city all the sighs/rising and falling
like sirens/thousands, maybe tens of thousands creating a
vast and lubricious symphony/a concerto/and in the secret
places/alleyways and back rooms at parties/some in crispy
beds/and some round backs of lorries or in graveyards/some
getting their oats before their time/by dint of threat/in
lonely fields/dragged there by snatch-crazed fiends.

LES: Digging in and hacking away like crazy robbers/smash
and grab of flesh/and tides rising and falling together/while
the mad moon/a giant's eye spying it all out/the
murdered and the robbed/and geezers out for bondage in
Earls Court/and in the night the steam is rising/from the
heaps of bodies twisted in shapes like vampires feasting on
their prey/and the cars passing/occupants all warm and
cosy/he's driving/Zappa in stereo/hand on knee/maybe one
will stop for me/and some delicious and horrendous
piece/swathed in filth-packed flesh will utter/can I give you
a lift young man/drooling sibilantly from scarlet lush-filled
lips/opens the door/smelling like honeysuckle in the dark
the hint of things to come/the promise of Elysium/and we'll
shoot off into the night searching for treasure.

KEN: But nothing/only the jeers of dawn carousers heading for
their unmade beds in Walthamstow and Leyton/reeking
stale beer and fish and chips/Fray Bentos pies from all-night
stands in Spitalfields/then home belching their unholy gut
rot into their scummy slags that hang around hair lacquered
like Brillo pads/and waking in the light of day/one white
arm/with digital/cheap one upon his wrist comes snaking
out the pit where scrubber lies a-snoring.

STEVE: And searching in his trousers for a pack of fags/start the
day in cough-wake/dragging ropes of phlegm/from vaults
well stocked within/blue smoke rising/while the sunshine
peeks reluctantly in/exposing a big juicy yellow pimple on
her back/comes then spewing through the radio some
idiot/so the day starts in a bath of rancid bacon and eggs.

MIKE: I'll get into my little bed/thus strengthened by steel for
the battle ahead/I'll drink a pinta/say my prayers/and wait
for mum to wake me in the morning/French toast and tea/I
double fancy that.

ACT TWO

Song of the Hoxton Mob. They march around the stage with East End macho-animalistic precision, jutting heads and threatening stares, to a drum beat.

CURLY: I'm known as the avenger/when
　　　　they see me they do quell/for
　　　　they see before their runny
　　　　eyes a short pathway to ultra-
　　　　violence/with a swift descent to hell.

　　　　They scare before they get here/
　　　　they tremble at my name/to look
　　　　upon my face is quite enough to
　　　　send them packing off before
　　　　they've time to clench their
　　　　sweaty fists to deal out pain.

　　　　I'm known as the avenger/and they
　　　　seek to claim my crown/but the
　　　　hardest villains are the ones that
　　　　soonest/come tumbling down.

　　　　So come on boy/I'm waiting
　　　　I hear you're on your way/
　　　　I'm hungry for the blood of
　　　　victims/I need another jerk
　　　　like you/a mama's boy to slay.

MIKE *jumps into a pool of light and becomes a Cockney Lenny Bruce for five minutes.*

MIKE: Every day in the morning – while the sun rose like a
　　　　biscuit behind the glue factory/quivering in the smoke/I'd
　　　　get up at seven to go to work mum packs some
　　　　sandwiches/which would get soggy by the time it was
　　　　opened/I would crush myself in the tube and others behind

me would crush and we'd all get crushed together/which
was all right if you happened to have your leg wedged
between the thighs of some radiant fair-skinned blushing
and divine darling but not if some stinking gentleman from
an exotic country of the East was breathing the shit he calls
food all over your face/and as the doors slid open this
composite mass of sludgy flesh would wobble like a wall of
jelly/and some schemer would put a foot in the door and
attempt to weld himself into the compost heap quivering
together/on the Piccadilly Line poo! who farted? was it you?
I'd read the latest filth scrawled up when the doors open no
one would move to let anyone in/we were staunch allies in
our square foot of space/the doors shut and the pack got
squirmier/I was thinking about that bundle all the while
and making horrible little flickers in my mind about the
outcome/eyes staring into their daily tits that they'll never
feel only ogle/hands would wander about in the pit of hell/
old ladies gasping their last breath/glaring at some young
sod in a seat/and umbrella stuck up your ass/fags stubbed
out in your face/and the ads advised you on the merits of
speedwriting/revealing some grotty slag smiling deliriously
like an insane gorilla/while chewing on an improvised cock
drawn by a future Picasso/and I stare all the time at the ads
like it was a meditation/while performing frottage against a
piece of taffeta/lovely/working as typist in Oxford Street/oh
no, don't get out yet/I'm not there yet/you may not be dear
but I am!/oh sod it/Oxford Circus/and the train heaves us
like a bad case of diarrhoea/then I'm channelled up the
elevator still holding my dangle/and briefcase with the
squashed-up sandwiches/churned up like the debris of
human rejects/bits of machinery on the conveyer belt going
back for repairing/or destroying/and I hoped I'd see that
bird again/she was lovely with great gooey eyes/maybe I'll
wait for her tomorrow/wend my way to my office in Bond
Street where I was a managing director of a firm of
wholesale jewellers/flogging pearls out of a suitcase in
Oxford Street for Xmas (genuine three-strung diamanté
pearls/a quid/with beautiful engine-turned, bevelled

edges/come on don't just stand there/gentleman over
there/lady over there/watch out there's a johnny/nip into
Woolie's or the ABC for a quick cup of bird
vomit/travelling salesmen swilling down some unidentified
goo/grins stitched to their unfortunate faces/collapsed
spine/frayed cuffs and souls/and breath to fell a dragon/I
saw a geezer shove his fork into a pie at one of these filling
stations/of garbage manufacturers/but it was empty except
for a mouse that was curled up inside with a happy look on
his face/sleeping/and he didn't want to disturb the mouse
like he thought it could have been a pet/since a lot of these
chain cafés have a lot of mice around/so he took it back/this
mouse has eaten my pie miss/she said/this waitress who was
slithering around in the dead grease/with bunches of
varicose like gnarled roots on her pins/says: what and it's
still alive!/I'm glad something likes our pies/here never
mind the humour I want another pie/he was sweating now
since he used this day's voucher up/she says I'll send it back
to the makers and if they find it faulty they'll refund your
money/but this didn't solve the problem/and he screamed
that they didn't need to send it back/the evidence is there in
the mouse/so after all the rhubarb and shouting/he's kicking
up a big pen and ink/the manager comes sludging over/a fag
hanging out of his head/and one off his ear/and one up his
ass no doubt/so this greasy manager comes wiping his
fingers on his apron/since he'd been making ham
sandwiches/had distinguished himself in service by cutting
the thinnest ham in the world/and was straightaway
employed by Forte's/so here he was and said if you make a
fuss like this in a good British café/three million men fought
the Second World War on food like this/so the salesman
bowing to his superior size says all right/and the manager
seeing that the salesman had calmed down said/was there
something he could do for him/and the salesman
brightening up a bit says/perhaps you could warm the
mouse up please/certainly sir, right away sir, came the
immediate response/but the mouse sussing something is up
with all the movement going on cocks an ear and runs down

the waitress's leg/she screamed/farted loudly enough to
shake the windows and slides over on the greasy
floor/keeling over a table on the way down/whose aged
occupants were shocked into a sudden coma/well after that I
didn't fancy going back to that café any more/it's all true/
don't look at me like that/I'm worried about that
fight/anyway I gave up flogging bent gear in Oxford Street
after that/they say there's a big future in flogging
magistrates with bags over their heads/they pay well.
(*They all mime a tube in rush hour, the words of the* CHORUS
syncopating with the train:)
ALL: Breakfast, shit, work, lunch, bed.

*Back on the tube or walking the streets – slow motion – best on the
tube – only a few strap-hangers or passers-by become* MIKE'*s friends.*
LES: Hallo Mike/I wish you luck for tomorrow.
MIKE: Thanks.
RALPH: How do you think you'll do?
MIKE: Very well thank you/how's your mother?
RALPH: She's OK.
MIKE: Still washing your knickers?
RALPH: No fear/I send them to be read by a fortune-teller.
LES: Are you scared?
MIKE: Not a jot/not a jot.
LES: I bet you are.
MIKE: How much/wanna see my pants?
SYLV: Don't go Mike/they're goading you on.
MIKE: What are you doing on the Piccadilly Line?
SYLV: Giving head to accountants in the rush hour.
MIKE: That's not very nice/is it?
SYLV: I waited in all day for you Sunday.
MIKE: I had things on my mind.
SYLV: That's what they all say.
MIKE: Who's they?
SYLV: I wish I knew.
STEVE: Going down the Royal tonight?
MIKE: I can't/gotta preserve my strength.
STEVE: Pity, we had something really dishy lined up for you.

MIKE: Keep it warm for me under the grill/I'll be back.

STEVE: You hope.

MIKE: What do you mean?

STEVE: Oh words words words.

MIKE: They're trying to undermine my fierce endeavour.

KEN: Hello Mike/coming for a ride up West?

MIKE: Not tonight Ken/not tonight old son.

KEN: Who's going with you Mike?

MIKE: I'll go alone unless you want to hold my coat.

KEN: Do me a favour/I wouldn't go down there for all the
    salmon in Wentworth Street.
    (*All except* MIKE *leave the train.* PEARL *and* SID *get on.*)

SID: You could have been an accountant or a manager of a string
    of menswear shops.

MIKE: I'd rather be bounded in a nutshell and count myself
    king of infinite space.

PEARL: Michael, my son, my joy and pride/jewel of my loins/
    apple of my eye/the light of my life/the be-all and
    end-all/the sun in the morning and the stars at night/where
    are you going my son?

MIKE: For a fight to the death/a battle of honour/destruction of
    a monster/to kill the plague/to slay the dragon/to defend the
    weak/to prove my worth/to destroy the mighty/to avenge
    the dead/to annihilate the oppressor/to be a mensch/to have
    a punch-up.

PEARL: Well wrap up warm/it's bitter out.

SID: Come on, Mum.
    (*They leave the train.*)

MIKE: Stars hide your fires/let night not see my dark and deep
    desires/maybe I'll go dancing after all to keep my mind off
    it.

The CHORUS *is seated as in a dance hall.* MIKE *takes* SYLV *into the
centre of the floor. Gradually the others dance around them, holding
invisible partners.*

MIKE: Do you wanna dance/I took her on the floor/the crystal
    ball smashed the light into a million pieces/a shattered lake
    at sunrise/the music welled up/and the lead guitarist/

plugged into ten thousand watts zonging in our
ears/callused thumb whipping chords/down the floor we
skate/I push her thigh with mine/and backwards she goes to
the gentle signal/no horse moved better/and I move my left
leg which for a second leaves me hanging on her thigh/then
she moves hers/swish/then she's hanging on mine/like I am
striding through the sea/our thighs clashing and slicing past
each other like huge cathedral bells/whispering past
flesh-encased nylon/feeling/all the time knees/pelvis/
stomach/hands/fingertips/grip smell/moving interlocking
fingers/ice floes melting/skin silk weft and warp/blood-red
lips gleaming/pouting/stretching over her hard sharp and
wicked-looking Hampsteads/words dripping out her red
mouth gush like honey/I lap it up/odours rising from the
planet of the flesh/gardens after light showers/hawthorn and
wild mimosa/Woolie's best/crushed fag ends/lipstick/
powder/gin and tonic/all swarming together on one heavenly
nerve-numbing swill/meanwhile huge mountains of aching
fleshy worlds are drifting past each other holding their
moons/colliding and drifting apart again/the light stings/the
journey is over/the guitarist splattered in acne as the rude
knife of light stabs him crushes his final shattering
chord/the ball of fire stops/and I say thank you very much.
SYLV: OK.
MIKE: Speak again, bright angel.
SYLV: I fink I'll have a gin and tonic.
LES: You're avoiding your destiny by diversions.
MIKE: Tomorrow and tomorrow . . .
SYLV: I waited for you all day Sunday.
MIKE: I had something on my mind.
SYLV: Come on home/I'll cook you a plate of spags.
MIKE: I'd rather eat the air promise-crammed.
SYLV: You must be starving.
MIKE: I'm preparing myself for the battle on Sat.
SYLV: Will you come over after?
MIKE: Yes long after/if I am here.
SYLV: Are you scared?
MIKE: Not a jot.

SYLV: Why are you so mean/you told me you loved me once.

MIKE: You were the more deceived.

SYLV: Heaven help him.

LES: Oh blessed Mike/why art thou not in constant training
    for the event?

MIKE: How do you know what I do all day/who watches my
    mental exercises/detects the secret plans I make/an armoury
    of weapons/stored in the forceful regions of my brain/I'll
    hypnotize the beast/and psych him out/drinks all round.

LES: Here's to the end of the Hoxton King.

RALPH: Destruction of the stinking dragon.

STEVE: The ogre falls.

KEN: Hideous and most sweet revenge.

LES: No more trembling in the strasser.

RALPH: Pull the birds we like.

STEVE: Safe conduct to the supermarkets.

KEN: Unimpeded entry to the Essoldo.

LES: Sleep tight at nights.

RALPH: Noisy mouthpieces/no frighteners.

STEVE: No knifing from bumper cars at Battersea.

KEN: Our motorbikes safe from slashing tyres.

LES: No more dreaded smells.

RALPH: No more terrified cats.

STEVE: Shaking OAPs.

MIKE: The Hackney marshes.

ALL: The Hackney marshes.

PEARL: You could have been had you tried/a manager/a
    solicitor/or even a representative of a firm of ladies
    underwear manufacturers/your uncle would help you/I'm
    sure you would have liked getting into ladies
    underwear/look at your cousin Willy.

STEVE: Wife – three kids – responsibilities.

KEN: House in Colindale.

SID: Detached.

LES: Mark 2 Cortina – £15,000 a year.

    (*They follow* MIKE *as he runs away from the train of
    responsibility that pursues him, and they circle stage and sit.*
    MIKE *whips round and makes a speech to the audience.*)

MIKE: Why should I yoke myself to 9 to 5/stand shoulder to
shoulder with the dreary gang who sway together in the
tube/or get acquainted with parking meters/be a good
citizen of this vile state/so I can buy an ultra-smart hi-fi and
squander fortunes on pop singles/what do you do at night
between the sheets but dream of mortgages and oh dear the
telly's on the blink/we're going to Majorca again this year/
you who've never raped a virgin day/with adrenalin assault
upon your senses/but aggravate your spine to warp/while
grovelling for a buck/or two/smiling at your boss/and spend
heart-wrenched hours at the boutique deciding what to
wear/ragged up like Chelsea pooftahs/or chase some poor
mut/on Sundays/mad keen to commit some GBH upon it/
and birds like screaming hyenas with teeth and scarves
flying/make your usual boring death-filled chat in smelly
country pubs/with assholes like yourself/no that's not for
me/I'd rather be toad and live in the corner of a dungeon
for other's uses.

The HOXTON GANG *with their leader,* CURLY. *They appear to lean
against a lamp post, each facing out, like four gargoyles, a hard light
from overhead.*

CURLY: Night and silence/that's what it's all about.

BURT: You're right Curly/oh son of night – the atmosphere is
double-strong/star-filled/the perfect evening for a fight.

PAT: It's what you need/a cobbled street/just wet a bit/to give a
little image of a broken moon/a yellow lamplight/flickering
a bit/still lit in gas.

REG: The echo of our studs on lonely streets/the smoke of
cigarettes/thickening in a blast of light/like fiery dragons/in
our lair we hover/smelling blood/our leathern wings
glistening in the dewy air.

CURLY: The odd moth hanging about/and eyeing up the
scene/banging his fretful wings/oh let me in it says/to the
hungry flame.

BURT: Then out he goes/like a light double-choked/to be so
scorched up.

PAT: Right burnt up he was about it.

ALL: Laughter – cackle – silence.

CURLY: In just such a manner doth our fretful moth of
Stamford Hill/bang against the light that we give out/he
wants to be let in/and then . . .

PAT: Phhht!

CURLY: We wait/we've time/I don't think he will be late/I sense
him now weighing up the scales of chance/thinking thick
regrets/and oh what a mug am I, swallow it, he thinks, turn
yellow/at least you'll keep your face/the one the birds do
like to chase/you'll lose the other/the one you'll never again
show to mates.

PAT: He's as chicken as a chicken coming to a fox/his pants hot
lined in shit/I hear/that fear has wrenched from out his
guts.

BURT: He does it to be king of his bankrupt domain/to cancel
out the bum he is at home/so he can spout out to the world
that he's got clout/and make the teenyboppers moist their
flowers/and holler, oh Michael/so he can stand up West and
join the firm of grievous/rape/robbery and death/solicitors to
the realm.

PAT: He desperately wants his diploma/and that is you/to launch
him on the path of hate/that's lined in gelt and not a caper
down the Ly/a bundle for a laugh/but turn pro/that's his
game.

CURLY: I'll not disappoint him/I am guaranteed against
default/reckless in my desire to give value/fear no marks
upon my well-worn face/have nought to save/but welcome
all/I'll make love to him/my caresses will start their long
journey in hell/he'll not see it coming/only feel/I'll embrace
him like a hungry bear/my hands will find his body's
treats/and practise on his bones/we'll dance and then I'll
look into his eyes/wet with tears of thankfulness/as I do
renovate the house he lives in/he'll whisper like a gasping
lover/to the background of splintering sounds/as he hears
the music of his body's walls snap and crack/his heart will
beat a terrible drum/and want to burst to spread some
numbing death relieving darkness/so come on scum.

The café of Mike's mates.

LES: Two teas, Joe.

JOE: Sugar?

LES: One, ta.

RALPH: Got any sandwiches?

JOE: Sold out.

RALPH: Do you suppose it's possible to organize one?

JOE: Not now.

RALPH: Why not?

JOE: Because it's late.

RALPH: Ah, go on, don't be a fat pig.

JOE: Closing.

LES: Sod you, you slimy middle-aged fart.

RALPH: I hope you starve/the time will come when nobody
    comes in this dung heap and your family is condemned to
    catch rats to eat/while your children crawl in lice and your
    wife's hair falls out/may your daughters be gang-raped by
    Blacks/and your house burnt down with your kids
    screaming/while you sit here counting your gelt you
    scheming piece of dogshit.
    (*Record on juke-box: "You are the sunshine of my life".*)

JOE: All right I'll make you a sandwich/what do you want?

RALPH: Roast beef and coleslaw in toasted brown.

JOE: Just watch it/next time you'll go too far and say something
    you'll regret, OK?

STEVE: Half-hour to go/Mike cut his hair and greased it/he can't
    grip that/so as to introduce his knee upon Mike's head.

KEN: That's shrewd.

STEVE: We should have been there/we should.

RALPH: Then why weren't we/case the others jump him if he's
    out in front?

STEVE: Dunno.

RALPH: You're his mate aren't you?

STEVE: Well, so are you.

RALPH: Yeah.

STEVE: He's mad to go/what does it prove/to swallow it's no
    shame/we know Mike's tough/ignore those bums/that's
    what I say.

KEN: He'll swallow nothing/so he'll taste nothing bitter in his
     mouth like us/he goes because he has to/and for us/you
     know that's true/he goes for you!

SID *comes downstage, alone.*

SID: Once in Soho, a while ago, round the back streets/walking one
     night to catch the tube I wandered round the alleyways/a
     saunter for no reason but to stretch my pins/up in the window
     was this bird/a right cracker she was/I stopped and caught her
     staring down/a red lampshade that tells all I don't know why/
     but I was tempted by all the mysteries that glow foretold/I
     pretended to be staring in the shop below/transistors and
     electrical equipment/but up above was the socket I needed for
     my plug/a card said "Sally, two flights up"/I found myself
     upon the stairs/grim smells and rot/knocked on the door.

SYLV *at home pouring a drink, upstage.*

SYLV: I hate to drink alone/sometimes I must/it quells the energy
      I have which I'd rather spend on someone/some him/or him/
      he leaves me with it bottled up and spare/I drown it out/my
      youth is going up the spout/in love that's wasted/I hate to
      stay in alone/how many others are like me/alone in
      boxes/waiting for someone or the phone to ring/what's the
      use to wait/and if he does/a thing of shreds and patches.

SID *and* PEARL *downstage.*

SID: So well, I knocked upon the door/and this scrubber opened
     it/looking like nothing on earth/while far below it was a
     mystery/I thought/she smiled/and showed a gap or three/the
     rest was black/and on her face a cake of slap/one inch thick
     at least/I thought I can't do this/I had my wages in my belt/
     not much since times were hard/and mum needed the gelt/
     for rent and clobber for the kids/a coat as well/but even so I
     couldn't now turn back/I hurtled through a quick time
     for . . . don't ask/it cost a bomb.

PEARL: You promised, Sid, you said I could have a new coat.

SID: And found myself outside the electrical store/and nothing
     to show except a rancid shag/and wages short/felt sick and

empty/I couldn't buy my wife her winter coat/I sacrificed
my wife for that/I'm sorry Pearl, I said, I earned a few bob
less/you'll have to wait a week or two/felt real vile/she said.

PEARL: You promised Sid/you said that I would have a new coat
Sid, this winter/that's what you said.

SID: I know/don't go on/don't start nagging/I sweat out my guts
for you/I break my balls that you should not go short.

PEARL: Don't shout in front of the kids!

SID: I sit down by a bench all day/machining trousers for five
bob/and dust choking my lungs/and the noise of the
machines/you wouldn't believe it/and fifty in a room/ten
pair of pants a day/I slog to make/cut and trim/then throw
them to Greek to finish off/and put a fly in/and at the end a
Mick to press them/I got callused hands already from the
shears/a spine that's curved forever/and a cough that can't
be cured by all the medicines in the world/that's known to
man/to make a haven for my family/which is a little
heaven/so don't get on my tits.

PEARL: OK/I'll wait/sure I can wait/wanna cuppa?

SID: I wouldn't say no to nice cuppa, Pearl.

PEARL: I hope Mike's OK/I haven't seen him since yesterday.

SID: Does that surprise you/you look surprised as if that's new/
that he appears when you see him and not before/a plague
he's been to me/(*to himself*) . . . it cost a bomb.

PEARL: What did?

SID: Nothing, what did I say?

PEARL: You said it cost a bomb.

SID: Oh I was miles away.

In the café, or MIKE *walking. The following can be said either by a
chorus of* LADS *or by* MIKE, *lecturing the* LADS' *still faces. For
continuity,* MIKE *should be alone.*

LES: At least the joy of being strong.

STEVE: Of owning your own body.

RALPH: Your capitals, your guts.

KEN: In your hands you hold the pleasure or the pain of the
Western world.

LES: Hands can be the instrument of life.

STEVE: Or death.

RALPH: What's it to be?

KEN: Either way you have to choose.

LES: You who watch and never had a choice.

STEVE: You took the only way.

RALPH: How many times did you want to lash out?

KEN: Give vent to what you felt?

LES: The bile that's choked within.

STEVE: Instead ate humble pie.

RALPH: How often did you want to impress the missus?

KEN: Be Charles Atlas and kill the dragon like St George?

LES: And how often did you tremble in your socks?

STEVE: Afraid in case you lost . . .

RALPH: Or broke a nose.

KEN: Ooh, painful.

LES: Damaged an eye even.

STEVE: There's lots to fear.

RALPH: And swallowed some offence.

KEN: A mouthful of slagging vile.

LES: And wished next day . . .

STEVE: When safe at home that you had taken chances.

RALPH: A memory to chat about on wintry nights to all the kids . . .

KEN: Of how you were a hero.

LES: For a while.

STEVE: Never mind, you made a bomb in wholesale and made a fortune in the market like a lucky Joe.

RALPH: Beneath it all you wanted at some time to be a hero with your dukes.

KEN: To emulate John Wayne.

LES: Or other prince of celluloid.

STEVE: Because that's your courage that you stake.

RALPH: Your guts you gamble on the street.

KEN: Opposing some hard tearaway.

LES: And whip him.

STEVE: That's worth a lot.

RALPH: You know it in your heart.

KEN: How many carry an emblem of some shame . . .

LES: Some insult not yet purged away . . .

STEVE: That gnaws your very vitals?

RALPH: You forget, you say! Ignore that cad.

KEN: Don't get mixed up with riff-raff, darling, says your dolly bird.

LES: You jump into a cab.

STEVE: Agree with her . . . they're not worth it.

RALPH: Ignore the mob.

KEN: Yet underneath it all you wish there were a Bruce Lee tucked away.

LES: Or a Mike.

STEVE: Instead you pour a drink and gas about an incident at school when for a minute you stood up to wrath.

RALPH: You play the incident again.

KEN: And yet again.

LES: Re-run the entire scene.

STEVE: Imagine what you would have done . . .

RALPH: Had you the chance again.

KEN: Let him say it once more, you utter in your dreams.

LES: Too late.

STEVE: And if you had the chance again . . .

RALPH: Wouldn't it have been the same?

KEN: But knights are born not made.

LES: The others stand round and watch.

(*They march off as tight group and comfort* MIKE.)

MIKE: See ya tonight then.

RALPH: Bird's in the club.

STEVE: Don't feel well, Mike.

LES: Gotta fix me scooter.

KEN: Me mother's sick.

MIKE: Don't let me down, will ya?

ALL: 'Course, Mike, yeah, etc.

Sylv's pad.

SYLV: What are you doing here?

MIKE: Aren't you pleased to see me/I had to see you/wish me luck/I got a little flicker in my guts/I must confess.

SYLV: Of what?

MIKE: Doubt and sick all mixed.

SYLV: Then don't go.

MIKE: Have to.

SYLV: Why?

MIKE: Sylv, the Fates have wrapped me up/to be delivered this night/I've got to go/revenge is one/strong one for a pal/as for the rest/what else is there to do/sure there is always a day that has to come/that you would much rather avoid/postpone/and send a card/forgive me/but/I can't make it this week/you lie in bed and sweat/hope the daylight never comes/it's not tomorrow any more/it's now/the readiness is all/but after if I'm still around/I'll pop on over.

SYLV: I wanted much more than that/the occasional hallo love and how are you/you busy tonight shall I come round/to sit and wait is not my idea of paradise/in case you decide this is the night that you decide to come/and what do we do but pass the time until it's time to go and "see ya! Be in touch!"/I'd like to be there for a man/who lives for the moments/so I can live for the moment too/when we can meet/and protect that which we grow together within me/ not here love – here's a ton/go get it fixed/a hundred quid to kick it out/buy back the space I'd rather fill/a hundred quid/to kill/that's easy for the man in love with death and pride/you are more keen to see your Hoxton pal so you can be a tearaway/the King of Stamford Hill/if you gave me as much as you give him/I'd be so happy/if I obsessed you half as much/you'll give each other all the thrills you are afraid to spill on me/you are in love with him not me/so go enjoy yourself/be free/far easier for a hand to make a fist than hold it open for a caress/easier for you to smash yourself into his body than to mine/to make yourself into a ball of hate wound up/so you can hide yourself from what you fear/be a hard man/cause hard covers the soft/the soft that's underneath is what you fear/my woman's body tells me/is soft to make things grow/its softness breaks down your rocks/can destroy you like water wears down stone/go to your lover Mike/go, and don't come back/go/be alone/and who will put you together again when you're a pile of broken bones?

MIKE: Thank you very much/I'll bear in mind all what you
said/I spit out all my angst/confess my guts/wished I had bit
my tongue first/before I let those soppy words crawl out my
gob/I had a shred or two of doubt I do confess/and that is
all no need to make a song and dance/accuse me of some
vileness in my act with you/it takes two to tango/don't
forget that/anyway I'm here aren't I/I come to you don't
I/there's no one else/at least . . . you get the best/sometimes
the worst/that's what it's all about/that's how it goes/that's
what they spout in church even/for better or for . . ./I'm
sorry you don't find me your ideal/you never will/you birds
have scored into your head/some geezer all identikit/a
mister right/but they never can and never will fit the little
pictures that you make/so without more ado/I'll take my
leave of you.

Street.
MIKE: Didn't wish me luck even!
　　I dunno/I'm all alone, that's how it goes/my mates have
fled/left me for dead/and most pernicious woman left me
too/I need a friend/need someone/something/just to tell it
to/tell me I'm OK/I'm good/nah I don't need/anyone/I need
revenge/that's something to get on with/that's a start/don't
take away my *raison* dirt track/don't take away my art/I'll be
myself again/but now a numbing sickness is sliding down
my gut/I'll force it back/I clench my fist/it feels like jelly/
like a baby's paw/if only I had the strength of a kitten I
could win/I see myself reflected in a windowpane/a death's
skull stares me in the face/where is my resolution/where the
spleen that had me think I was the king of the master race/
bearded with the sweat of fear/a demon came and sucked
my blood/they sense victims and hover like bats/the filthy
beasts/that's all right/who ever felt happy before a fight/you
go in sick but once you start and get the first sting in/your
face you then forget your problems/like an actor on the
stage/scared shitless in the wings but once he's on then he's
the king.
(CHORUS *rushes on—reflects* MIKE's *walk upstage.*)

OTHERS: (*At random*) You can do it, Mike.
    Didn't wish me luck even.
    How do you think you'll do?
    He's mad to go.
    No blood of mine.
    But hers . . .
    One minute, Mike.
LES: Hackney marshes.
    (*The* CHORUS *leaves the stage.* MIKE *is alone. He acts the battle.*)
MIKE: He hits me with a hook/I'm down/a bolt to fell an ox/ crumbles slow/then smashes me with a right/and now/I sway/a drunk looking for a hold/a volley a hard straight comes whipping out/smashing home/I go down slow like the *Titanic*/but grab hold on the way/and drag him down leaking red from all openings but still I hold him/close/he can't be hit/too close/and with my almighty arm I lock his neck into a vice/where do I get the strength/the brute's amazed thinking it was all done/but finds his head being smashed into the wall/but like he's made of rock/he twists himself from out my grip like some mad demented bull and snorts screams and kicks but by this time I dodge the sledge hammers and hold him at bay/alive again as if the blows have woken me from some deep sleep/I'm myself again/we move and circle/it's quiet as the grave/all tense waiting/the beast kicks out and hard/I grab a leg/and down he falls/hard/but with almighty strength the brute is up again/ sneers and foams/and rams his fingers round my throat/grips hard/the others round about/screaming/kill the bastard/tear out his guts/and rip his balls off/I pull off his wrist and then we twist/fall/rolling/each trying to find a hold/and lashing out from time to time/knee/elbow/head/ boot/whatever finds itself unoccupied and free for service/we break away and stand streaming like two dragons breathing flame/fighting to the death/each waiting for the other to move/still/just the sound of breath/then in the beast goes and fast and throws himself on me like to annihilate me once and for all/I go flying back thrown by the mass of

hate and crash both down in a welter of struggling seething
flesh/twisting foaming heaving screaming/I'm stomped
on/sounds unearthly are heard/I fear it must end/and bad/
he's on my chest/his fist drawn back/one horrible almighty
gnarl of bone and brought it crashing down on to my face/
pow and then again pow and now again pow/I can hear the
sickening crunch/but I protect what how I can/draw energy
from the deep and thrust my hand up underneath his jaw/
with the other I smash it home/the brute stumbles/pulled
off balance/my face is crimson blind by blood/I wipe with
one hand/I'm upon him now spraying his blood on both like
we were swimming in it/this time grip his throat and hold it
fast/tight/tighter/after long time we topple over/again/rise
slow like prehistoric monsters/the beast screaming/words/
spitting out/no meaning/splattered curses/he bows like to
pounce again/I then kick/it lands home dead square in the
face/then follow up both hands working like pumps/like you
never saw.

CHORUS: Pow-pow pow-pow-pow/pow-pow-pow-pow-pow!
MIKE: But you wouldn't believe the strength of the
brute/inhuman like/grinning like a gargoyle/he stands there,
says come on do something/and charges again/I can't
believe/as if my own powers mean nothing/see hopelessness
and fear now flooding in as fast as strength is flowing out/
we grip each other for a hold/to throw one or the other
down/but I'm losing all belief/I'm down/as if it's better
there/just lie covering my face/I'm kicked pow/once twice
pow/feebly attempt to rise pow/kicked down/the fourth time
in his glee/too keen, he misses/slides over on the blood
slippery deck/heavy as lead/I climb up in agony/but do not
miss the chance/to connect the monster's head with a bone-
shattering well-aimed knee/it stops him dead/it looks
surprised/astonished/and for luck/throw all my weight into a
right which crashes open all in his skull/out go the lights
pow/the Hoxton King keeled over/toppled/crashed down/in
one terrible long rasping blood gurgled moan/then it was
over/he twitched/raised his head/spewed between his bloody
teeth the words/"Nice one"/then lay quite still/me

yelling/the lads about looked sick and pale/were shattered in
their souls/and thought the future black/I wiped the blood
away/put on my coat/they parted quietly for me when I
left/I staggered into casualty at London Hospital who fixed
me up.

*Gang as group like cheerleaders. They trot around the stage to give
him a hero's welcome.*
MATES: Well done and welcome home/you done us
    proud/terrific/so we heard.
KEN: Report was trumps.
RALPH: From far and wide.
LES: Your triumphs sung to the four corners of the manor.
STEVE: You look a mess.
ALL: But hold your head up/you're the ace.
MIKE: Oh yeah/my nose is broke/my lovely profile's gone.
RALPH: You'll get it back.
STEVE: You'll look better than ever once it heals.
KEN: Don't you fear.
LES: Sensational it were, I swear.
RALPH: My heart was out there for you . . .
STEVE: Stomping in my chest . . .
KEN: Like fifty insane drummers.
LES: When you got up and curled your right . . .
RALPH: I said a little prayer for its journey into space.
ALL: He didn't know what year it was/he didn't care!
MIKE: So where were you, deserted me ye men of little
    faith/all mouth and trousers when it comes down to the
    crunch/you could have shown a face at least to plonk your
    minces on the scene should tricky business raise its ugly
    face/instead you wait for news of my impending fate/it's
    over now/it's done/so what's it all about/I've had enough of
    this/I'm out.

*MIKE creeps into his house – enters Pearl's and Sid's room for the
first time.*
MIKE: Hallo.
SID: What the . . . ? Look at your face.

PEARL: Mike, oh God, what happened to you?

MIKE: I had a fight . . . but I won . . . I did it.

SID: So, look at your, what do you want/a medal?

MIKE: No/I just wanted to tell you/it's the last one I'll have.

SID: So tell me something new.

PEARL: Leave him, Sid.

SID: He's proud/he comes in here to tell us he's proud.

MIKE: It was hard/yeah I'm proud/his gang did up little Harry.

SID: Don't give us this talk/this time of night/your gang
warfare/a gangster I've got and he comes in yet like he's a
hero.

MIKE: I just wanted to talk to you.

SID: So/you've talked.

MIKE: I needed to tell someone.

SID: So you've told me/what do you want us to do?

MIKE: Nothing, just nothing you miserable lump of
complaint/that's all you've done all your life/what else are
you good for/nothing/and you give nothing/I've listened to
your miserable snivelling complaints for years/I've had
enough of you/a swollen bag of useless opinions like all the
old sods like you.

PEARL: Don't aggravate your father/his ulcer's killing him/go to
bed/wash your face and go to bed/you don't look well, son.

MIKE: Ma/you've tied yourself to a lump of concrete/and it's
sinking into the swamp.

PEARL: And who's complaining?

MIKE: I am!

PEARL: Don't worry about me/go to bed.

MIKE: OK.

(MIKE *exits.*)

SID: Tell him in the morning to go/he's got to go/I for one can't
take any more/so tell him/Pearl he's our son/but he's got to
get out of this house/I can't take any more of it.

PEARL: I'll tell him.

SID: Make sure you do.

PEARL: I will/I said I will.

SID: He's got to go somewhere and do something/but I don't
want him around any more/I'm sorry.

PEARL: In the morning I'll tell him to go.

SID: Don't soften up and change your mind.

PEARL: I'll tell him it's best for all of us if he went.

SID: You'll tell him that.

PEARL: Yeah.

SID: Cause this can't go on like this.

PEARL: I know that.

SID: Then we can have a bit of peace in our old age.

PEARL: Yeah.

SID: You know what I mean.

PEARL: Of course/I'll tell him in the morning/I'll tell him he must find somewhere else to live and not come back this time.

SID: I did my best.

PEARL: Yeah.

SID: Didn't I? . . . You sound as if I didn't well/didn't I or not/ did I show him those ways?

PEARL: No, I did.

SID: What you talking about?

PEARL: From me he saw that not to fight was to give in/he saw that I never fought back/so he had to.

SID: You'll tell him in the morning to go!

Epilogue.

MIKE: I can't go on like this/look at me/my nose is out of joint/I can't see straight/I've got no job to speak of but I won/I won/I beat the beast/with my own two hands alone/I reached out and defeated what they feared/I conquered my own doubts when sick inside/that's great/so tell me where to go and what to do/and what's the trick that makes for happy days and nights/the fireside and mates around for Xmas/the wife cooking a bird/a baby going gaga/the colour telly on/the Daimler shining round the front/what did you do to get it/do you thieve/stay on at school/or work your loaf/inherit some cosy chunk of loot from papa/go on tell me the trick/what's the clue I need to know some answers/or I'll make my own/you who sit comfortably at home/who wake up with a grin and toast and eggs/tell me what you do and how you do it/never mind I'll find you out/I'll get the wind on you/I'll break out of this maze/and sniff around your pen/I'll be the beast you fear/until I get an answer/straight up I will/you had me do your dirt/and stood around to gape/while I put down the fears that kept you sleepless in your beds/there'll come another beast/for every one you kill/there will grow another head.

Further epilogue.
PEARL *and* SID. GANG *as respectable people stand behind them.*
SID: Don't you worry/we did what we could/he's not so bad/a little wild/but soon he'll find his head/and if he don't/well then/others will help/there are the courts/police and magistrates to guide him on the way/prisons to help persuade/and keep society safe/so all in all he's no real threat to you and me/we keep our noses clean/pay the rent and rates/smile our social smile/and leave when they call time.
PEARL: But he's your son.
SID: No son of mine.

Blackout.
Faces of characters.

LUNCH

CHARACTERS

MAN
WOMAN

Lunch was first performed on 19 December 1983 at the King's Head, London. The cast was as follows:

MAN	Ian Hastings
WOMAN	Linda Marlowe
Director	Linda Marlowe

Empty space bathed in a cool white light – faint music being played – strange discords which italicize the action from time to time. A beach anywhere. A WOMAN *sits by a table, she is facing the sea, a deserted beach café.* MAN *enters frame from left to right. He sees her – enormous reaction – freezes. He seems unsure whether to come or go. So just stares.*

She senses him behind her – they hover thus for a moment, she aware, still, eyes chasing from left to right.

He, as if to pounce – stealthy, but still, eyes boring into her – two animals caught in each other's fear. He edges forward as if casually, carrying a briefcase.

MAN: (*Aside*) Beautiful, oh she's beautiful – who is she waiting
    for – no one for me – ? Her neck soft as a baby's thigh – I
    could bite valleys out of it. I could . . .
WOMAN: (*Aside*) Turn around. . . ? No, that's an
    invitation – who is he – throbbing silently as a shadow
    behind me – burning holes in my back.
MAN: (*Aside*) To go up to her – gently slide up like a ghost . . .
    kiss the nape of her neck – then she'd murmur softly – soft
    as bees and offer her mouth to me like a hungry bird.
WOMAN: Poor beast . . . he's dumb . . .
MAN: Hungry bird . . . mouth open . . .
WOMAN: Shy – he wants to – talk – he should . . . (*Turns her head
    quickly.*)
MAN: (*Startled*) Right through me she looked . . . straight
    through me . . . I didn't exist . . . I was a tree.
WOMAN: He could . . . he should . . . his mouth . . . aches to
    speak . . .
MAN: JAWS LOCKED! . . . TONGUE ROOTED INTO MY MOUTH . . .
    granite . . . speak now, or remain mute . . .
    dumbstruck . . . Dead
    (WOMAN *moves as if to leave.*)
    No, no not yet! Budge not thy heavenly bum . . .

petal-lined, proud, strutting . . . Not yet . . . Heat-filled
bitch of a thousand juices! Not yet.

WOMAN: Too late . . . too late, soon . . . Quickly!

MAN: Walk past . . . casually sit . . . Speak! Shout!? No, I'll go
away . . . coward . . . Oh, you terrible priapic
coward – cock hard . . . gut soft . . . coward.

WOMAN: I can't say anything . . . can I?

MAN: Too late – too late – the heart aches – the shock would be
too great.

WOMAN: A pity – he was nice.
(*She has begun – so she must go.*)

MAN: What words ensnare? – captivate – enchant – rape –
suggest – amuse – interest – stun . . . (*To her*) Lovely day!

WOMAN: Yes – yes it is really lovely!

MAN: So many lovely days we're having – all at once.

WOMAN: Suddenly . . .

MAN: You would think it could be summer.

WOMAN: You would think so.

MAN: Yes we're lucky.

WOMAN: Certainly we are.

MAN: Do you mind? (*Seat.*)

WOMAN: Please do.
(*They briskly examine each other.*)

Alternate:

MAN: Blue eyes nice – I like
that – fullness in lips,
soft . . . skin smell, legs
crossed, skirt short . . .
darker recesses leading to
the various succubi and
incubi swarming in her
panties, those gardens of
cotton roses, a child
wandering through hot
gardens . . . those
smelling summer
times . . . I love her . . .
(*Easy movement.*)

WOMAN: (*Rapid*) Brown eyes
nice – hair dark
soft – hands strong
big . . . worrying
thoughts . . . swimming
nose, eyebrows, teeth,
mouth – avaricious –
devouring – like to
be – now – who is
he – what does he
– how does he –
bird-like – hawk-like
predator . . .

MAN: The sea is calm today.

WOMAN: I like it like that – the way it churns in – chasing itself – not boiling or seething . . .

MAN: Dissolves on shingle as if grabbing with large tentacles . . .

WOMAN: A pile of coins – like coins slipping through its fingers as it retreats . . .

MAN: Tentacles not fingers . . .

WOMAN: It moves – a wave moves like a mole under the water . . .

MAN: Or a rat under the carpet . . .

WOMAN: A long wave pushes, pushing until it collapses . . .

MAN: A fatigue of spume – spent froth white spume . . .

WOMAN: A long last gasp, phew!

MAN: Look at the sea! Like several hurdlers . . .

WOMAN: Racing – legs outstretched . . .

MAN: Relay runners, passing baton . . .

WOMAN: OH! Now they're collapsing.

MAN: The other runner is taking it – now he too collapses.

WOMAN: I like the sounds – lik-lak against the shingle.

MAN: He's sliding back into the arms of a dying wave.

WOMAN: They greet with much murmuring . . .

MAN: More a barely audible whisper – not close friends . . .
   (*Pause.*)

WOMAN: I like the hurdler best – I can see that.

MAN: I like watching them race to the finishing line.

WOMAN: The sun's high in the sky – so heavy . . .

MAN: A fine breeze slides across our faces like cobwebs . . .

WOMAN: The sound of the sea is like whispered thunder . . .

MAN: Thin orgasmic little gasps . . .

WOMAN: That rock looks like a huge claw – frozen as if it pounced on what it shouldn't.

MAN: Little wavelets bob and bow at its base.

WOMAN: Unctuous, spittle, boot-licking – toe-cleaning.

MAN: I thought I felt the earth shift.

WOMAN: It's a lovely day.

MAN: I think you're lovely – too. (*Aside*) HER BUTTOCKS ARE SAILING ON TO MY HAND LIKE A TEA CLIPPER ON ITS MAIDEN VOYAGE BOUND FOR THE ANTIPODES.

WOMAN: (*Shyly*) Strange thing to say on a beach – in your shirt and necktie.

MAN: ". . . rich and modest, but asserted by a simple pin."

WOMAN: "They will say: 'But how his arms and legs are thin!' "

MAN: "Do I dare
   Disturb the universe?"

WOMAN: "In a minute there is time
   For decisions and revisions which a minute will
   reverse."

MAN: My name is Thomas – Tom to you.

WOMAN: Oh, good – you could have been Bert – I'm so
   glad – I'm Mary.
   (*Silence*.)
   You're not on holiday? What do you do?

MAN: (*Aside*) Desperate finger acrobatics . . . cruelly exposed
   electric thigh encases, sheathed . . . my birthday
   present . . . (*To her*) Selling mostly.

WOMAN: Mostly selling. . . ?

MAN: Space – mostly, I sell spaces of space, acres of nothing.

WOMAN: (*Disappointed – only a travelling salesman*) Oh . . . !

MAN: (*Aside*) She said – her face collapsing – rephrasing
   herself – adjusting its concaves and shades – refocusing
   past me . . . she crosses her legs, quick sound of surfaces
   abrasing – signals of soft regions, the promised land . . .
   Boredom seeps through – vinegar through milk . . .
   "Oh!" – a collapse of the lungs – expiration of interest.

WOMAN: (*Gentle tolerance*) I'm sorry – I didn't mean to sound
   bored.

MAN: (*Quick aside*) She said, sounding bored.

WOMAN: More surprise really at selling nothing – how can you
   sell nothing – a salesman sells something – he must do . . .
   mustn't he? Something tangible – tactile?

MAN: I'm different, I sell the promise of something – the
   intangible mystery of an empty space – pure white virgin,
   untouched, waiting for a buyer to claim – to insert his
   identity, his wares . . . his amazing declarations . . .

WOMAN: A trade book . . . ! A trade book! You sell space in a
   trade book?

MAN: I promise trade in a space book.

WOMAN: How, promise?

MAN: When the book is full – when the white spaces are
bought – those infinite columns of expected wealth – I sell
the book.

WOMAN: To whom?

MAN: To them – to the clients themselves, the space buyers, so
they can gaze at themselves immortalized forever in block
letters – electro-type on quarto double-weight.

WOMAN: Lovely!

MAN: Yes . . . when the space is bought we go to
press – printing blocks set up, letterpress, text, matter of
context, put out first proof, check it . . . supplement the
appendix . . . print a duodecimo for special customers then
rush it out.

WOMAN: Exciting!

MAN: They open their books greedy yellow fingers . . .

WOMAN: Like fat worms?

MAN: Yes! Search for their spaces to see themselves described
forever in cuneiform characters – they like that . . .
Cigarette?

WOMAN: Thanks.

MAN: Do you want to buy some space?

WOMAN: Me?

MAN: How many of you are there? Yes, you.

WOMAN: (*Simply – wishing it were otherwise*) I have nothing to
sell.

MAN: Hmmm . . .

WOMAN: *Have* I?

MAN: (*More edge*) Hmmm – you could have – find something
– everybody's got something – some one thing – even the
successful have got something . . .

WOMAN: All I have is a name.

MAN: That's all you need – sell that – have a half-inch single
column, just your name in uncial lettering – you'll excite
their imaginations – they'll create dream worlds containing
their idealized female – suiting every situation . . . you'll
fulfil their fantasies, become a mind-real, homogeneous.

Flicking through the hardware section they'll come to your name sitting there like an unfulfilled hope . . . the ink of your nomen stinging their pupils – gently grazing them with mesmeric fantasies – they'll know you in a thousand different ways and shapes, hundreds of colours, textures, smells . . .

WOMAN: (*Smiling*) My name will do that?

MAN: Their minds will do that – but your name, your explosive sibilant sigh will ease the first scab off those old love wounds.

WOMAN: I'm not sure – no, that I want those fat-fingered men dividing me up in their nasty abattoirs – taking me to pieces, examining me . . . imagining me . . .

MAN: You'll feel nothing – not even the tick under the skin as imagination catches desire by the tail.

WOMAN: I will, I'll sense . . . things . . . hundreds of little rays eating me up – my name belongs to me . . . I'll sense things – silent buzzes in the air – hovering invisible gnats . . . biting . . .

MAN: (*Quick aside*) Sensitive, sentient being, a mare trapped in a spider's web – a diastole in the heartbeat . . .

WOMAN: Revolting men, fat, wheezing behind desks in dirty offices . . . Ugh!

MAN: Clean mostly – sterile bright, shining world – the men fractured into brackets, parenthetically courteously explaining, or else in italics "No, thank you . . . we've all the space we need, thank you, you're welcome, thank you . . ." At five o'clock the exodus – they stream out like diarrhoea . . .

WOMAN: You sound like high pressure – hissing from cracked pipes.

MAN: I'm no pressure – I dissolve into fat and slide under the door – staining the concrete stairs on the way down – those thousands of white – dirty – grey concrete stairs that have gnawed my feet away – choked on the dust – fine dust that concrete secretes – the salesman's disease – bang-bang, up the stairs then slither down in a visceral pool of grease dragging nerve endings, plasma and intestines . . . re-form

on the pavement – plunge the eyes back in – the shirt has
dissolved into my flesh – become an outer skin . . . Recoup
in the ABC – salesman's filling station – pump in the hot
brown bird vomit – the others are just sludging in, their
faces slapped puce with rejection, the waitress, sliding
around the dead grease – falling apart at the seams, slithers
her knotted varicosity towards me and for a treat smashes
some aerated bread down my throat which dissolves into a
dust, white dust – like concrete dust, atrophying delicate
nasal membranes . . .

WOMAN: Don't you like your work?

MAN: Love it! Every moment, every earth-shattering
cosmological moment of it . . .

WOMAN: Even your dissolving agony?

MAN: That especially – you know the thrill of exploring this
fascinating city – meeting all those interesting
people – several square feet of flesh float up to you – not to
you directly but somewhere adjacent – dabbling in your
circumference . . . polite neatness glazes back at you, and
you shuffling sweaty lump – lift broken, spine snapped, eyes
at twenty-five watt, glint stumpy teeth, not exactly a smile
more a grimace of pain at the halitosis in your breath
escaping between your teeth like pistons . . .

WOMAN: (*Sickened*) I must go – but it's been nice talking to you.
(*She whisks herself past him. He jumps up and pins her
violently against the table.*)

MAN: (*Continuing*) . . . he may even buy some space to escape
your trajectory of rotting plumbing but usually the
protective secretaries have warned him of your
arrival – "He's tied up, in conference" etc. – they nose you
crawling up the stairs – they're ready – alert as vultures . . .
willing you out but wanting to tear you to pieces – behind
the door other creatures are lurking, grey-faced salesmen
with smiles stitched on to their faces hovering like bats
waiting for you to go . . . Trembling lest you take an
order . . . eyes bulging like grapes . . . order books stained
with dead egg yolk the memory of which long since
mercifully obliterated by some tired old intestine . . . so I

come here for an hour to look at the sea, to escape from it –
Oh, by the way, have a sandwich. (*Opens his briefcase.*)
They're really lovely, and you have a choice – Oh come on,
they're beautiful, made with my own hands, which should
add to the excitement . . . Go on please.
(*In persuading her he has spilt sandwich on her lap.*)

WOMAN: Oh dear – I've just had it . . .

MAN: Cleaned? Here let me . . .

WOMAN: No, don't, you're making it . . .

MAN: Worse? I'm terribly . . .

WOMAN: Sorry? Never mind – I must be off anyway.

MAN: Better still – have some soup – it's delicious like Grandma
makes it. (*Takes out bottle.*)

WOMAN: (*Rising*) No! Just leave me alone, will you?

MAN: Sit down! I'm not finished. (*Aside*) Tension's up, she's
become an ice lolly in a whirlwind.

WOMAN: I'm late.

MAN: Sit, animal. To heel! What is this, a cabaret? Go? Is that
what you do? Where are your manners – you call the act and
then walk out – what? You can't like the service? The
sandwiches? Me? All three? In that order – I'm not so bad
really, times are hard in the trade but things could be
worse, you could have done far worse, you should see some
of the casualties wandering around here playing pocket
billiards, but as long as you've got a pound in your pocket,
you don't have to ask anyone for nothing as my mother
used to say . . . a shine on your shoes, a nice cutaway collar
on a van Heusen shirt, you can sit in the Golden Egg, have
a nice cup of coffee, a chocolate éclair, hold your head up
and be a gentleman . . .

WOMAN: Goodbye then.

MAN: Aaaa . . . ! Wait!

WOMAN: I'm late . . .

MAN: Please . . .

WOMAN: I don't want any space.
(*He collapses in chair.*)

MAN: What do you want?

WOMAN: Nothing.

(He walks over and kneels at her feet.)

MAN: I'm here.

(He puts his hands over her calves – she does not move – they remain silently.)

WOMAN: No thanks – but thanks all the same.

(She attempts to move but he holds her legs firm.)

MAN: What's that mean?

WOMAN: No – that's what it means.

MAN: *(Imploring)* Two minutes more – I have something to tell you – marvellous wonders!

WOMAN: I've heard it – entertaining it's been – but I must go please – please let me go, please . . .

MAN: Don't you like me?

WOMAN: *(Weary)* Me . . . ? Like you . . . ?! Don't . . . !

MAN: What were you waiting for?

WOMAN: No one – I like sitting here – alone – that's how I like to be sometimes, I just sit here looking at the sea . . .

MAN: You were waiting! Yes, you were – I smelt your heat from across the beach. Your scent hung in the air like a pollen count – it commingled with the salty ozone and fish and sea, lost itself, but my quivering nostril located your particular waves – hound-dog-like sniffed it out, untangled it from the smell of fish and hamburgers fried, candyfloss, fags and dead sharks; located your special delicate whiff and zoned into it like radar. You were twitching for me, for somebody – yes you were – what did you expect, Gregory Peck? Or do you like the drama, the chat? It gives you satisfaction to be chatted to – sense of adventure – dallying with the mad unknown – weird stranger on the beach . . . picked up . . .

(She attempts to go.)

No, stay, you don't want to go back to that bare room, vinyl-lined, do you . . . ? Alone – rattling round four walls except for those flying ducks flight-frozen in dust, your frustration banging off them, the walls not the ducks, the street full of couples sliding happily across your windowpane past dead flies (feet saluting heaven) . . . and you pacing around waiting for the phone. So you come here for your adventures – to dispel the agony or share it.

WOMAN: I have a home and a husband and no agony to share –
so let me go!

MAN: Ooh! A husband – but there's not the joy there was,
eh . . . ? So you compensate a little – inject the marriage
with a little spice to hold the structure together – I know
how you feel . . . the same body lying next to you night
after night after night – over and over again – it's sickening
isn't it . . . ? Search for the mad adventure of the first or
second time when you clawed each other apart as if you
could discover, as if you could wrench the secrets from that
ticking body – oh the terrible adventure of a first time . . .
Hurtling yourself at that marvellous machinery of
joy – assaulting, exploring its labyrinthine pleasure
grounds . . . Satin-lined, lovely warm corridors, armed
with rubber teeth and special scented sauna rooms and ice-
cream parlours . . . Don't you wake up with that snorting
creature and for a second imagine that he could
be – something – one else . . . All this fantastic energy
burning holes in our stomachs – all this shock tissue dying
from unuse . . . Don't you ever want something else? Yes,
that's why you come here. Here I am for you – here you are
for me . . .

WOMAN: Nothing . . .

(*He walks over and kneels at her feet.*)

MAN: Here I am.

(*He puts his hands over her calves – she does not move – they
remain silently.*)

WOMAN: You're not looking for me – you're looking for *it*! Any
it, like a dog you sniff all the lamp posts . . . panting,
licking anything that comes your way, if it moves, sniff it,
that's you, you salesman of nothing, you canine groper.

MAN: (*Aside*) Calves hard as sculpture, warm as roses . . .

WOMAN: Wherever you drag your failure you leave a penetrable
whiff, a sour old fag smell – a whine, a hum of decaying
dreams and festering ambitions – it lingers in the air like
BO.

MAN: (*Aside*) The blood's pumping – veins enlarging – shifting

masses in the flesh stir with life – the shoots begin to
move – the earth aches – the ache enlarges. THE EARTH
BEGINS TO SHIFT!

WOMAN: You demonstrate your wares like rotting garbage – you
woo like a leper – your expressions are the buried side of a
stone, moving with strange fetid life – dark, decayed, small
scraping movements in the earth – odd creatures black and
runny . . . or crawling . . . what the cat paws but carefully
with distaste –
(*He puts his hands round her hips; holding her more and more
tightly – she remains passive.*)

MAN: (*Aside*) Skulls pounding – a rat-tat-tat murder – blood
soaks the brain, lids twitch and pupils dilate, skin stretches
taut inside, everything taut, tight inside, outside – drums
banging lubricious symphonies – trembling cadenzas –
everybody take your partner – follow the rhythm,
together – millions dancing the maniac jerk, the viscous
spasm . . .

WOMAN: (*Not moving*) Take your hands away – your grimy,
greedy little fingers – take them . . . *ay-way* . . . every pore
a little hungry sucking nerve-centre drinking sensation . . .
go away . . . your little slimy worms annoy . . .

MAN: I'm going – I'm going – I'm going, I am going . . .
soon . . .

WOMAN: Now.

MAN: Soon – you *can* go – yes, you can go . . .

WOMAN: Now.

MAN: Soon, soon, soon – then you *can* go . . .

WOMAN: Now – now let me go – *please* now –

MAN: Soon, *please* soon – go soon – not now – not yet. (*Rising
tone*) Not *now* – not *just* yet – not *so* soon . . .

WOMAN: (*Weakly*) You're defeating me!

MAN: No quarter – burst through . . .
(*Pause, during which she collects her strength for the climax – to
hurt and be hurt. She beats him frantically.*)

WOMAN: Bite me. Bite snake! Bite loathsome! Draw
blood – drink, drain me – you! You are a loathsome
beast – searching and sniffing – your antennae alert as

stretched tendrils – sensing out, sending waves creeping
through the air, crawling stains of blood through laundered
sheets . . .
(*He puts his hands round her neck and gently squeezes.*)

MAN: I want to murder you – draw your life out into me . . .

WOMAN: Murder me – you foul joy – you conquered repugnance!
(*Blackout. Music . . . the amplified sound of flowers opening.
Their voices could be prerecorded.*)

MAN: I tore into her body's haven
    ripped off rose-petalled flesh
    sucked from a host of seething fountains
    her sweet rich sanguine life

WOMAN: She said
        devour me all
        leave not one sliver
        not one small clue of silken down
        with tenderness he tore my heart out

MAN: Then bit into the puzzle of a frown
    imbibed, engulfed, devoured her . . . all!
    even her arms, long white and thin

WOMAN: No fragment left he of me sacred
        no faint opacity of skin
        not one square white unstained by him
(*End of blackout. When the lights come up their clothes and
physical state could suggest a swift fuck.*)

MAN: Anyway, so I suppose . . .

WOMAN: What do you mean?

MAN: It was nice . . . yes . . .

WOMAN: Nice . . . ? For who?

MAN: Not you . . . ? Not nice for you . . . you mean?

WOMAN: Like a fire engine, putting out . . .

MAN: A fire? You! A fire, *you!*

WOMAN: You died from exhaustion on the trek – you didn't
rouse a twitch – or heat a pale flush . . . "no quarter"
"burst through"! You couldn't burst through an ice-cream
in a heat wave!

MAN: That black hole in your face squares into a tunnel of
love . . .

WOMAN: You are a dirty little man.

MAN: Crawling words creep out like spiders from your ancient gob . . .

WOMAN: I do *believe* you dissolve into fat and slither under doors – you look like something that dissolved and recomposed with the bits and pieces off the floor – misshapen – lumpen – that's failure for you – a man who can't sell nothing – or make *something*!

MAN: Aah! What do you know you lump of fornicatory stew, dolloping up bits of your overcooked goo . . . what do you know! Who can linger on that – it . . . it (*Imagines her body – miming*) falls apart in your hands – fingers don't find resistance – strong, muscular, cellular resistance of filth-packed flesh, no they just sink into you – loose masses of wobbling, like a pack of dirty stories in aspic . . .

WOMAN: You're a real funfair comic – you're the woodlice that one finds buried in bars telling the dirty stories you'll never play in – stand in! Understudy!

MAN: Never play in?! I star in my own melodramas, long runs, you one-night stand you!

WOMAN: I have a husband, I am to him, my husband, a veritable drama of sensual events . . . that's what I am – a panoply of exquisite variations . . . To him that's what I am, besides him you dissolve – you're androgynous, on you it's an ornament!

MAN: Your husband never makes the love to you you think he makes, but via you he is loving. Whilst you pant together exchanging your sweat and stink, his imagination's taking him to dreamland – you're just his launching pad, his receptacle for his journeys into outer space where his dollies lie waiting for him – his icy maidens fixed like cold glittering stars ready to perform wonderful feats of endurance . . . but wait until their light dies – just wait until then – because so will you . . . a pack of memories, marriage . . . other people's . . .

WOMAN: You are a poisonous spider – you really are . . . poisonous. Yes, you even look like one – a crawling garden spider, no not garden – the thing that darts out of dirty

cupboards, that you step on . . . FAST – yes, you do . . . My
husband loves me – yes he does – he loves me and soon it
will be time to go home and prepare his supper – he comes
keenly – lovingly in – expecting little kitchen noises and
smells . . . he brings the cold wintry air in with him . . .
smelling of train fumes and of Aqua di Selva – all fresh – a
rough chin tickling me, his smells reassuring me – all
familiar . . . and he loves me – really and hugely LOVES, and
I make him his favourite meals his mother once made him
and we eat and watch TV – not plays, or quiz shows, serious
things, *Man Alive*, *Panorama* – we discuss them afterwards
and he writes long eloquent letters to *The Times* about
injustice – but they never publish them . . . He's full of
goodness – exudes it like vapour – it clings to the walls of the
room – every room . . . it reaches into the grain of the
furniture – becomes part of them, part of me, so secure,
cocoon-safe . . . six-ten each evening, his tinkling key in
the lock, his hat on the stand faintly grease-stained – his
himness coming in – hard, masculine himness wrapping the
house with blankets of love . . . and just so he comes in the
door, he whistles, so as not to alarm me, so I know it's
him – not anyone else, but him – not a burglar or a
murderer, a little whistle (*whistles three notes*) and if I'm in
the kitchen I whistle back so he knows I'm there – not
gone – not died – a victim of GBH or gang-bang angels
leather-winged – but there in a perpetual way, like he faces
me square on, direct and coming to me, always to me . . .
even when not facing me he's coming to me, his thoughts,
murmurs, hungers, desires, always reaching me and mine
him, so our invisible webs are always gripped even miles
apart . . . I finish his sentences, he collides with mine,
anticipate his wants – I don't need anything else – don't
certainly need you . . .

MAN: No – I'm not a whistling Aqua di Selva-ed square-on . . .

WOMAN: No – you're not square-on – you're oblique – you enter
from the side – or the back – like an unseen fist – one only
sees the shadow before impact, clenched malice – you –

MAN: No, malice clenched I'm not – a caressing angel more like.

WOMAN: A fist – all of you, a fist, to strike – you caress with your
     fists to be ready – curled ball of furious venom – be
     anything else, you couldn't.

MAN: I'm not a fist – my hands are soft – they caress – protect
     DELICATE THINGS . . . Make flowers grow, life appear, make
     people happy, women giggle, cats purr, dogs wag . . .

WOMAN: Goodbye then finally.

MAN: Goodbye.

WOMAN: Yes, goodbye.

MAN: Goodbye – go on . . . be home for six-ten – don't break
     your cocoon, soft-silky warm places should be
     protected – mad, you are, to be doing with me.

WOMAN: I'm sorry.

MAN: What sorry! Sorry that – sorry for . . . ? What?

WOMAN: Sorry – just sorry.

MAN: That's me, yes, oblique, the darting rat in the corner of
     your eye . . .

WOMAN: (*Encouraged*) Be careful . . . you're . . .

MAN: (*Showing his hand*) No fist – look (*A silence – he and she just
     look uncertain.* WOMAN *slowly takes one hand in hers.*)

WOMAN: You've uncurled . . .

MAN: The sea's stopped moving, the earth pauses . . . for a
     moment . . .

WOMAN: The tide has gone far out . . .

MAN: It begins to return, lovely, I think you are . . .

WOMAN: The sea is lovely and you . . .

HARRY'S CHRISTMAS

The play is a monologue spoken by HARRY.

Time: Christmas. Place: A room.
HARRY *is counting his Christmas cards.*

Four, five, six. That's all. That's the lot . . . but there's some
from last year . . . let's see. (*Looks through last year's.*) I could
maybe add a couple . . . No you shouldn't do that . . . that's
silly . . . to make it look better . . . who cares? But it looks a bit
thin. YOU WORRIED WHAT PEOPLE MIGHT THINK? Yeaah! PEOPLE
WHO MIGHT DROP IN, MIGHT THINK, POOR HARRY, NOT VERY
POPULAR? Something like that yeah. LOOK AT THE SIX CARDS AND
PITY YOU? Maybe, yeah maybe. THINK, WHAT HAS HIS LIFE
BEEN – TO HAVE SO FEW CARDS? Maybe, yeah. WHO AND WHAT DOES
HE MEAN TO THE WORLD? Christmas tells you . . . that you have
sweet FA. Christmas says that's your standing in the world . . .
you score six miserable Christmas cards . . . Christmas to make
you feel like you don't exist . . . Christmas is like an avalanche
coming . . . you want to run away, but you've nowhere to
hide . . . I hate it . . . Nah! It's not so bad . . . that's average for
the season. But if I don't get more than six I'll definitely add two
from last year . . . maybe three. Ha ha, maybe I put up all last
year's, nah, the last five years' and have a bonanza. Ha! Ha! Gee
you're popular Harry! Why save them? They're nice though,
some of them. They remind me. It's a piece of memory. (*Looks at
cards.*) Mum and Dad, brother and aunty . . . one from work and
two from . . . friends. Those two . . . not seen them for
years . . . but every year they send a card and I send one
back . . . so they know I'm still alive . . . and the message is
always the same: "Give us a ring sometime." But I don't, because
they don't want to hear from me . . . not really . . . but it's nice
to rub the old memories up a bit and then they get a card
back . . . but not before. I wait and if they miss a year then so
will I. But they only missed one in the last ten years. I had moved
so it got misdirected or lost or is still seeking me out . . .

four days to go. I might get four more . . . That's all I need,
four more to make it ten. That would be acceptable . . . that's a
reasonable bottom line because three are from your family and
don't count, so six more would be very good but even two would
be tolerable . . . But one more . . . or none . . . that's
impossible. No, ten would give me a real stake in the world and
as Santa comes and delivers all the goodies just a couple more
down my chimney. What are stinking cards anyway . . . a
desperate message of "I love you; please love me" and hang up
all your stupid cards on a line in the lounge . . . prove how you
are loved . . . I don't care . . . I don't send cards unless I get
them . . . I don't want to get cards from people who would
never dream of sending me a card but for the fact they received
mine, so I get an obliged card . . . so that doesn't count. I want
cards from people who want to send me a card. Not obliged but
I send a card back if my old friend sends me one. Yes. But I
don't feel obliged. Maybe I should send loads. Like putting out
lots of lines and getting a bite . . . maybe just flood the world
with cards for every human being who touched me . . . or I
touched . . . all the ones of the past . . . the history of my
being . . . then they would send me one and then we'd continue
by picking up the threads . . . that dropped . . . like a light
bulb with the threads broken . . . the tiny filament . . . so no
current pours through . . . so a card would be attempting to
light up the filament and make the connection. And if they reply
then it lights up. Too late now. Only four days to Christmas. I
used to get more . . . in the past. I had cards . . . sometimes a
dozen . . . once I got twenty . . . yes. That was a record year. I
was working in an office and everyone felt they should send each
other cards. So it was a freak year but then it dropped back to
twelve and then ten then six or seven and so decreasing year by
year. Then, if my parents died I could only guarantee myself
four . . . even three. That's not so good . . . I'll put a few more
out for now. (*Puts four old ones out.*) WHY DID YOU DO THAT?
DOES IT MAKE YOU FEEL BETTER? Yes. IN CASE ANYONE COMES TO
VISIT? Yes, they'll see . . . HOW POPULAR YOU ARE? Not even
popular but normal . . . at least normal . . . like everyone . . .
not . . . LONELY, UNPOPULAR, UNLIKED, UNDESIRABLE,

UNBEFRIENDED, UNKNOWN, UNCARED FOR, UNINTERESTING . . .
UNBEING . . . No, I don't care . . . if I sent more cards I'd get
some more . . . I don't care . . . THEN WHY PUT UP LAST YEAR'S?
Ashamed for them. WHO IS THEM? YOUR LANDLADY, YOUR ONE
FRIEND, A VISITOR, A CHANCE CALLER? NOBODY CALLS YOU BY
CHANCE. Somebody may. I'm expecting someone . . . what the
hell . . . does it matter? (*Takes cards away.*) How stupid, how
foul . . . (*Puts them back.*) But they look cheerful. I don't
care . . . better make sure there isn't last year's date on them.
(*Studies card.*) "Give us a ring sometime." Hmmn . . . I didn't
ring the whole year . . . I thought about it . . . maybe I
should . . . maybe they'd even ask me over . . . Nah! They
make their plans weeks ago . . . those kind of people prepare for
Christmas like you prepare for war . . . or as a kind of obstacle
course . . . I don't care . . . so what's Christmas . . . another
day . . . where the non-beings get counted . . . you could vanish
among the mob the rest of the year . . . but now the mob
gathers its forces and flees and you're exposed . . . naked . . .
with your cards . . . not enough to cover your nakedness . . .
why join the mob . . . preparations . . . and stand in a queue in
supermarkets dragging home some dead poisoned bird . . .
Nah! Christ was born so I could count my cards . . . he came to
earth to make me lonely as a piece of shit that didn't go down
when the loo was flushed. Still, it might be nice . . . sitting
round a table and getting a bit pissed with the kids leaping
around and watching TV films . . . Nah . . . I could watch it at
Mum's. I'm sick of going to Mum's at Christmas . . . sick of
it . . . she's old and falls asleep in front of the telly so I end up
watching it alone . . . and then I go home in the evening and
end up watching more of it. Wonder if I should ring them . . .
just say I'm ringing cause you said, "Give us a ring
sometime" . . . so here's the time . . . "Happy Christmas" . . .
that's all . . . don't say, "What you doing?" or they'll think I'm
begging to be invited . . . no just "Wishing you a happy
Christmas" . . . they'll say, "Come over and have a Christmas
Eve drink" . . . no doubt they'll be having friends over. I
wonder . . . (*Stares at the phone a long time.*) DO IT . . . DOES IT
KILL YOU TO MAKE A CALL . . . EXTEND A HAND . . . MAYBE

THEY'RE LONELY TOO . . . MAYBE THEY NEED FRIENDS, SO LIFT UP
AND DIAL. THAT'S WHY THEY SEND YOU A CARD . . . THEY LIKE
YOU . . . YOU USED TO DO EVENING CLASSES TOGETHER BEFORE
THEY GOT MARRIED . . . THEY'D BE PLEASED . . . YOU USED TO
MAKE THEM LAUGH . . . REMEMBER THE STORY THAT YOU TOLD
ABOUT APPLYING FOR A JOB AS A SECURITY GUARD . . . YOU
COULDN'T GET THE BUTTONS IN THE UNIFORM AND SO YOU DIDN'T
EVEN START . . . YOU COULDN'T COPE WITH THE BUTTONS . . .
REMEMBER HOW THEY LAUGHED . . . GO ON . . . DIAL IT. No!
No! Don't ring in desperation . . . ring out of pleasure . . .
they'll hear it in my voice . . . desperation . . . it will put them
off. SO WHAT . . . PUT THEM OFF . . . YOU DON'T GET ANYTHING
BY BEING AFRAID . . . EXCEPT PEACE IN YOUR LONELINESS IN
FRONT OF THE TV . . . THE GIFTS FOR THE FEARFUL, YOU
FRIGHTENED LITTLE WORM. Yes, a worm . . . frightened . . .
they're together . . . and if they say, "Yes, come over" . . . a
single man . . . nearly 40 and still sees his mum . . . had a
woman once . . . as a matter of fact I had quite a few . . . years
ago . . . she still writes. (*Looks at the other card.*) "I hope you are
well" . . . Clara – Clara was nice . . . lasted six months . . .
pretty good . . . but she didn't send a card this year . . . not
yet . . . but left her address on top so I sent a card instead . . .
wish I had contacted her . . . maybe she's lonely . . . maybe she
never found anyone . . . but a year without a word. STILL YOU
COULD PHONE HER AND SAY, "MERRY CHRISTMAS, CLARA, COME
OVER FOR A DRINK." Yes . . . JUST A DRINK WOULDN'T HARM AND
CHEW OVER THE OLD CUD . . . SHE MIGHT LIKE THAT. She might
indeed . . . Christmas Eve, come over and split a bottle of
wine . . . NO, MAKE IT CHAMPAGNE. Champagne . . . yes . . .
why not! Hey, that's good . . . I'll do that. YES, DO IT NOW
WHILE THE SPIRIT IS UP . . . YOU JUST IGNITED A LITTLE SPARK
THERE. Keep it aflame . . . don't dampen it with doubts or
fears . . . like she might have a boyfriend or even a husband.
DON'T . . . YOU'RE DAMPING IT RIGHT NOW . . . YOU'RE PUTTING
OUT THE SPARK. No . . . No, do it now . . . just ring up . . . to
hell with the consequences . . . WHAT CONSEQUENCES . . . WHAT
ARE YOU TALKING ABOUT . . . YOU'RE ONLY ASKING HER OVER FOR
A FEW DRINKS . . . WHAT CONSEQUENCES? Like she thinks in two

years I haven't found anyone . . . or she thinks I'm still trying
to get her back or she'd be confused since it's been two years,
she'll think I'm desperate . . . to ring after such a long time . . .
"Why the hell is he ringing now . . . he's lonely and can't find
anyone else." NO! YOU'RE THINKING THAT . . . SHE'LL MORE
THAN LIKELY THINK, "OH, HOW NICE TO HEAR FROM YOU AFTER
ALL THIS TIME . . . HEY, WHAT A SURPRISE . . . SURE THAT WILL
BE NICE . . . A LITTLE DRINK AND TALK OVER OLD TIMES." NO
MORE THAN THAT. Even if she does have a husband she'll still
think, "That's nice" . . . people like to see old friends . . .
you're right . . . you're right . . . the spark's coming back . . .
I'll do it now! Right now. Clara . . . Oh, she was nice. A drink.
THAT'S RIGHT, DO IT NOW. But what if she has a husband and
says, "Can I bring him?" FACE THAT BRIDGE WHEN YOU CROSS IT.
Sure . . . bring him, it's still company . . . it's still living . . .
and talking and not watching TV. THAT'S RIGHT, SO PICK UP THE
PHONE. But . . . WHAT NOW, YOU FOOL? STOP DIGGING UP THAT
CESSPIT OF DOUBT. IT'S A BOTTOMLESS HOLE . . . YOU COULD DIG
THERE FOR EVER – SO LEAVE IT BURIED. Yes, but it has to be
worked out . . . come for a drink . . . but then she'll expect
others to be there. If it's the two of us or even the three it'll be
odd . . . if I say a drink there should be two or three others
there or it's a bit personal. SO WHAT? YOU WERE ONCE CLOSE
FRIENDS . . . LOVERS . . . SHE KNOWS YOU. But if there's no one
else she'll know it's because I'm lonely . . . or want to get her
back or she'll be uncomfortable . . . now if I could get two or
even one other then it was a Christmas drink . . . otherwise it's
a bit depressing just the two of us on Christmas Eve. YOU'RE
DIGGING A HOLE FOR THAT SPARK AND BURYING IT DEEPER AND
DEEPER INTO THE EARTH . . . GIVE THE SPARK SOME AIR AND
WATCH IT CATCH ALIGHT. OK . . . I know . . . but I have to
work it out . . . maybe ask the couple who said ring . . . and
her . . . then if both come it's like a little party . . . or leave
it . . . I'm confused. I'll ring the couple, then if they say, "Yes
we'll be delighted to come" I'll ring her . . . it's difficult with
women . . . they always think you want something out of them.
WHAT? FRIENDSHIP, COMPANY, WARMTH, DIALOGUE . . . ? SO
WHAT'S DREADFUL ABOUT THAT? HOW BAD THAT IS! That's **not** so

bad . . . I could ask her . . . just take the consequences of my
action . . . whatever happens . . . ring now. YES, RING NOW.
FORGET MAKING A STRUCTURE OF HAVING THE OTHERS OVER . . .
YOU JUST WANT A FRIEND TO SHARE A FEW DRINKS WITH . . .
MAYBE GET A BIT PISSED . . . MAYBE SHE'S ALONE AND DYING TO
SEE SOMEONE . . . HOW DO YOU KNOW UNLESS YOU MAKE THE
EFFORT AND BE BRAVE? Be brave, that's it . . . I'll ring now . . .
then if she says yes I'll call the others . . . if they can't
come . . . that's it . . . OK. She's here anyway . . . good . . .
(*Stops and looks at the cards.*) Oh, I'd better take her last year's
card down . . . I'll put some other cards up . . . say two or three
more . . . now that looks much better . . . I smoke a fag
first . . . Now. (*Picks up the phone and stares at it; starts slowly to
dial.*) I hope she's away . . . or not in . . . but I'll be brave . . .
be brave. (*Dials – it rings for some time . . . keeps ringing – puts the
phone down.*) Phew! She's not in . . . that's OK. I did it! I'll ring
later on. Maybe she's moved . . . so what now . . . I'll ring the
other people . . . but if they say yes . . . then I won't be able to
have a quiet drink with her . . . but that's not what I
wanted . . . I want others around to defuse the situation. WHAT
SITUATION? YOU LIKED HER ONCE. DEFUSE WHAT? WHY ARE YOU
DOING ALL THIS FOR HER? DO IT FOR YOURSELF . . . INVITE THE
COUPLE BECAUSE YOU WANT TO NOT BECAUSE OF HER. That's
right! I'll ring them and if they come that will be good. Now
they did say, even this year, "Why don't you ring us sometime?"
They were nice . . . we had some nice times. (*Dials.*) Oh God,
it's ringing . . . Oh God . . . what shall I say . . . it's still
ringing . . . Hello! Jack? Hello, Jack, it's me . . . Harry! You
know, from the institute . . . Harry Glebe . . . You sent me a
card . . . Oh, Barbara sent it! That's nice . . . well, it said . . .
both . . . of . . . Oh, she sent all of them . . . Ha! Ha! . . .
that's nice . . . that's really nice . . . yes, Glebe . . . sure, don't
apologize! I knew you'd remember . . . Oh yes, the kids
shouting in your ear and you couldn't . . . sure I'll hold on . . .
Oh, I'm sorry . . . you're in the middle of a kids' party . . . No,
just to ring and wish you a really great Christmas . . . Is
Barbara . . . ? Busy in the kitchen . . . uh huh . . . Hey! How
many kids you got? . . . Wow! three now . . . sure I can hear

them . . . Oh, I'm fine . . . yeah . . . sure I'll give you and Barb
a call sometime . . . when you're not so busy . . . Ha ha . . .
Yeah, in the new year. (*Sudden*) Sure . . . Oh, what are you
doing for the new year? . . . Lovely . . . Is it hot there now?
Wow! I must try that sometime . . . no, never been . . . no, it's
OK, Barb doesn't have to call back . . . you said ring sometime
so here it is . . . Ha ha! Sure, thanks and to you too . . . have a
good one . . . a nice Christmas . . . you got the whole family
staying . . . my God, yeah . . . sorry? . . . I can't hear . . . the
baby's crying . . . what? Oh, I remember Michael . . . he was
just born . . . three now . . . my god . . . yeah. He wants to
talk on the phone . . . he likes that, yeah . . . sure, put him on.
SHIT, WHAT AM I DOING HERE? LET ME GET OUT OF . . . Hallooo,
Michael . . . this is Harreeee . . . you having a lovely
Christmas . . . aren't you a big boy now . . . a big boy . . . big,
I said . . . big! What? What? Oh, you wanna bikey . . . oh ho
your dad will give you one . . . you're a big fella now . . .
fella . . . oh, never mind . . . CHRIST AND SHIT!! Whadya wan
for Christmas? A bikey, oh yes, of course . . . a red one . . .
now Mike, if you pray to Santa and say I'll be a good boy . . .
Goooood! (*Aside*) For God's sake! Oh, I'm sorry, Jack, I thought
he was still on the line . . . sure, you're busy . . . yeah, you
too . . . yeah, sure, will do . . . bye. SHIT! SHIT! SHIT! SHIT!

Lights fade to black, then come straight up again.

Three days to go and no cards today. Who cares? Do I . . . no
more work . . . for a week . . . so it starts . . . one, two, three,
four, five, six . . . still six. I'll put these others out in case she
comes . . . Clara . . . what about thinking of someone else?
Still, there's time. No one rang . . . yet . . . inviting me . . .
anywhere . . . still they all go to families . . . yeah . . . they
don't enjoy it too much . . . better off here . . . really . . .
watch a few movies and get pissed in front of the telly. Ha ha!
See Mum . . . she needs cheering up . . . lots to do really . . .
three days . . . Friday Saturday Sunday and then D-Day . . . I
don't want to be alone again . . . not again, not like last year! I
can't stand it . . . it mustn't happen! . . . I won't let it fucking

happen . . . No! No! No! No! No! No! No! THEN DO
SOMETHING ABOUT IT . . . RING YOUR FRIENDS . . . RING ANYONE
YOU KNOW. MOUNT AN ATTACK ON LONELINESS . . . KILL IT . . .
DESTROY IT . . . YOU HAVE TO MOUNT A MILITARY
OPERATION . . . NO ONE WILL RING YOU. Why? . . . why do I
know that no one will call . . . why am I certain in every cell of
my body that no one will come here . . . phone here . . .
because . . . because . . . WHAT? ANALYSE WHY NO ONE WILL
CALL YOU. Because they go off to . . . NO, THAT'S NOT THE
REASON. ANALYSE FOR YOURSELF WHY NO ONE WILL PHONE. (*Cuts
off suddenly as phone actually rings, snatches it up.*) Hallo!?
Oh . . . hallo, Ma . . . yeah . . . fine . . . I haven't rung? Oh,
it's a week already, yeah . . . fine . . . how's everything?
(*Pause.*) Then you should lie down . . . I know, you're sick of
lying down, then try walking gently around . . . go to the
park . . . yeah, it is a bit cold still . . . still the days are getting
longer now . . . yeah . . . what's the doctor say? Just to take it
easy . . . that's what you have to do, yeah, so watch the TV, put
your feet up . . . You're sick of the TV? Well, so am I, Ma. I'm
sick of it, too . . . yeah, I am really sick to death of it! . . . You
watch more than me!? Then you must be even more sick of it
than I am . . . ha ha! So discover something else to do and you'll
make a fortune . . . sure, I'm coming round . . . yeah . . . No!
I'm not being forced . . . I want to . . . yeah I will . . . no, I
don't feel obliged . . . I know I'm free . . . don't talk like
that . . . I come because *I want to I said!!* . . . Sorry . . . didn't
mean to shout, don't get upset . . . (*Pause.*) Ma . . . Ma . . . ?
You still there? OK. You got all you need? I'll bring something
anyway . . . what do you need . . . no, don't go out
shopping . . . I'll bring it . . . it's not a chore, No . . . I'm not
putting myself out . . . don't go out, you're supposed to be in
bed. For God's sake, I'll get the bloody stuff . . . no, I'm not
upset . . . cheese with the holes? That's all? You got the
rest . . . OK, then . . . maybe Christmas day . . . yeah . . . Oh,
nothing frantic, maybe some friends over Christmas Eve for a
drink . . . you know . . . colleagues . . . No, you wouldn't
know them, Ma . . . How's who?? I haven't seen her for five
years, Ma! Oh, for God's sake . . . so lie down and I'll bring

some stuff . . . yeah, the cheese with the holes . . . and some
new green cucumber . . . yeah, not if it's soggy . . . OK . . .
Benny Hill's on . . . OK. Watch it . . . OK. Ma . . . look
after . . . No, I don't need anything . . . the cat's fine. Ta da,
Ma. SHIT SHIT SHIT SHIT SHIT.

Lights fade to black, then come straight up again.

Two days . . . I don't want to analyse anything . . . why should
I? BECAUSE YOU'LL FIND THE ROOT OF IT . . . THEN YOU CAN TEAR
IT OUT LIKE A VERRUCA . . . YOU HAVE TO MAKE AN EFFORT.
Sometimes my whole body feels like one giant verruca . . . it
starts in my foot and grows larger, then there's more to cut out
and then it reaches my leg and then it takes over all of me and
then there's more verruca than me . . . so the only way is to cut
the whole thing out . . . and that's me . . . get rid of that. DON'T
BE STUPID . . . GET IT NOW . . . LOOK FOR IT AND PULL IT OUT.
Yeah . . . if I could find it. OK . . . I'll try Clara again. (*Dials – it
rings and rings.*) She's away or working . . . maybe . . . I could
call (*consults address book*) Annie again. She was nice . . .
yeah . . . we had some nice times together . . . but I don't
know . . . YOU HAVE TO . . . YOU MUST OR YOU WILL DIG A
DEEPER PIT FOR YOURSELF. OK. I'll try . . . maybe I should also
try some men friends. But it's not the same . . . they're both with
their women or family . . . or don't want to be bothered. WHY
NOT INVITE PAUL ROUND OR AL? I could . . . I could but I don't
feel right about it. WHY? THEY MIGHT BE PLEASED TO HAVE A
CALL . . . HAVE THEM ROUND CHRISTMAS EVE, THEN THAT WILL
BREAK THE ICE . . . SO MUM WON'T BE SUCH A CHORE. You have to
make an effort . . . an attack on loneliness . . . but Christmas
they all have arrangements. Wives . . . girlfriends . . . YOU
DON'T KNOW FOR SURE . . . MAYBE THEY'RE LIKE YOU . . .
WAITING FOR A CALL . . . MAYBE YOU'LL BE DOING THEM A
FAVOUR . . . CALL NOW! I don't want to call anyone . . . I'll read
or go to a movie . . . have a meal somewhere . . . time will
fly . . . why should I have to think of suiciding bits of my life . . .
time should be precious to me . . . it should be like gold . . . more
than gold . . . and I want to piss it away . . . my life is a . . .

stink . . . that nobody wants to get near. ANALYSE IT. No No! I
don't want to analyse anything. PHONE SOMEONE. No! I'm sick
of begging for a handout. FRIENDS. I don't even like Paul and Al
that much and even if they were free . . . what for . . . to stand
in the pub and tell jokes . . . why, I'm sick of that . . . I'm
lonely . . . I'm desperately sodden and need someone to
hold . . . that's all I want to do for God's sake. Hold
someone . . . what's to analyse, it's flesh and blood . . . some
warmth . . . just to hold hands and go for a meal. What did I
do . . . I don't care normally . . . I cope . . . but now I feel as if
the whole world was in some kind of conspiracy against me.
They're all holding each other . . . all grabbing on and holding
and kissing and climbing all over each other and having friends
round for drinks and answering the door and kids shouting and
making dinners and chatting but where am I in all this? DID YOU
MAKE THE EFFORT? DID YOU TRY? Yes . . . yes, of course I
tried . . . I went out with them . . . I made them happy
sometimes . . . we went to bed and sometimes it was OK . . .
but it always ends . . . it comes and goes like musical chairs and
Christmas is like standing as the music stops . . . and you're
without a chair not for a few seconds but for days . . .
Everybody is at a feast from which you are excluded . . . (*Long
pause, takes a cigarette out and dials a number.*) Hello . . . can I
speak to Annie? . . . Hi, Annie, it's me. Harry! Yeah . . .
good . . . great . . . What are you doing with yourself these
days? Uh huh . . . uh . . . huh . . . uh huh . . . no . . . no . . .
I haven't found anyone to match you! Ha! Ha! Ha! Have you ah
found . . . oh good . . . that's good, sure, it's good to . . . how
long . . . you've been living together that long . . . and he's
OK? Yeah, great . . . Oh, I dunno . . . looking at our old
photos and I thought what the hell . . . let's see how the old girl
is . . . you know. I know it was difficult sometimes . . . yeah,
but there were some good times . . . yes there were . . . Oh,
come on, Annie . . . everybody fights . . . but we had some nice
times . . . you don't remember . . . you focus . . . what about
the days we went to Bournemouth . . . and we didn't fight . . .
not all the time . . . so . . . I should see someone about
what . . . I'm OK! I don't need help, damn it! Well, not that

kind . . . I didn't depend on you . . . you were my ally. Sure,
friends . . . I got loads of friends . . . don't lecture me for God's
sake . . . you see, you're making me angry again . . . so I won't
ring . . . shit, I won't . . . why did I. . . ? To invite you over
for a Christmas drink, you pig. (*Phone clicks off.*) DON'T GET
INVOLVED . . . YOU SHOULD HAVE JUST SAID . . . COME ROUND
FOR A DRINK. Should I? Who gives a shit? Now who else . . . ?
(*Hears noise.*) The postman just dropped by . . . hold on
there . . . (*Goes to door.*) HO HO! What's this . . . another
card . . . Wa hoo! Who's a popular boy today . . . now . . . who
is this from? (*Opens it slowly.*) "Happy Christmas, just to remind
you that your subscription is due at . . ." Shit! Still, it makes
seven . . . that's better . . . it looks a bit healthier . . . I wonder
if Clara is back now . . . WHY RING ANYONE . . . WHY
BOTHER . . . PUT IT DOWN TO EXPERIENCE AND GO AWAY NEXT
TIME . . . JUST LIVE AND BREATHE FOR NOW. GO OUT, WATCH TV,
SEE YOUR MOTHER, DO THE SHOPPING, GET CAT FOOD, SMOKE A
CIGARETTE, GET PISSED, GO TO SLEEP, GET UP, MAKE A CUP OF
TEA, SMOKE A CIGARETTE, GO FOR A WALK, BUY SOME GROCERIES,
COOK A MEAL, HAVE A DRINK, SMOKE A CIGARETTE, WATCH TV,
GET PISSED, HAVE A WANK, SMOKE A CIGARETTE, GO TO SLEEP,
GET UP, WALK ABOUT, GET DRESSED, GO OUT, COME BACK, GO
OUT, COME BACK, GO TO SLEEP, WAKE UP, SLEEP, WAKE, SMOKE,
EAT, WATCH, DIE. SHIT SHIT SHIT SHIT SHIT SHIT SHIT.

Blackout. Lights come up again.

One day to go . . . no more cards today . . . still seven is
nothing to be ashamed of . . . maybe Clara's in today . . . she'll
see me I'm sure . . . Clara! . . . been drinking too much . . .
got black on my lips . . . look at me . . . forty, not
bad-looking . . . not fantastic . . . sure, there'll be lots of
women who would like to have a friend over Christmas . . .
think of all the thousands, the tens of thousands of lonely
women everywhere and I don't bloody know where they are . . .
wish there was a signal you could use . . . "Look at me, I'm
lonely" . . . I'm not bad . . . I've got arms and legs and a
heart . . . I've got all the equipment to do it with . . . I've got a

voice to say things . . . like . . . "You're really nice . . . I love you . . . I want to be with you . . . come on" . . . I've got all this body . . . all this shape . . . occupying space . . . and no one to give it to . . . all my hands and fingers and lips . . . all my arms and legs and thighs and mind . . . it's all here. (*Makes a shape with his arms as if holding a woman round the waist.*) This space to let . . . loneliness is like a disease or smell . . . when you give off a whiff it puts people off. Why did I get like this . . . tomorrow is Christmas . . . Christ's day . . . he came to give us love and everybody goes away and gives it to someone else . . . he came to say, "Share your love. Give it . . . take it . . . don't withhold . . . suffer everything" . . . what is it . . . "Suffer the little children to come unto me" . . . I'm one of them . . . I'm a child of his . . . so where's my crumpet for Christmas . . . who cares about crumpet . . . it's not about that . . . it's about something else. WHAT ELSE, WHAT IS THE ELSE? ANALYSE THAT. ANALYSE IT AND YOU'RE NEAR TO SOLVING IT. Solving what – what is there to solve? THE PAIN THAT BLOCKS OUT THE FEELING. What pain . . . it's all pain . . . pain came from somewhere, get rid of the pain and feeling floods back . . . like taking a thorn out . . . YES, THAT'S RIGHT, GET RID OF THE PAIN AND YOU'LL FEEL . . . ANALYSE IT. What? I don't know what there is to analyse . . . I'm lonely, that's all . . . how can I analyse that? BUT WHY? WHAT'S THE REASON? I don't know . . . who knows? It's bad luck. NO SUCH THING . . . YOU DON'T KNOW, THEN ASK YOURSELF . . . BEG IT OF YOURSELF AND YOU'LL DRAW OUT THE PAIN WITH THE BEGGING. Beg what?! Maybe I'm not interesting enough. TO WHO? TO YOU? WHAT ABOUT THE OTHERS – WHO ARE YOU TO JUDGE YOURSELF? They judge me! WHO ARE THEY? Them (*points to cards*) those cards are my judge, six miserable fucking cards . . . they are my witnesses with one from the Insurance Company reminding me . . . and the one's that aren't there . . . YOU DIDN'T PLAN . . . YOU DIDN'T TAKE TIME OR THINK OF OTHERS . . . YOU WERE INVOLVED WITH YOUR OWN PAIN AND IGNORED THE WORLD . . . YOU LOVED YOUR OWN LITTLE AGONY. I did? I sweat for it . . . I plead . . . I ask . . . I phone up . . . ONLY FROM PAIN . . . NOT FROM PLEASURE . . . IN DESPERATION AT THE END. So what should I do if not now . . .

wait until I'm happy enough to crack a few jokes . . . what
now . . . wait for the pain to go and sit in an empty room
studying my pain with the TV on . . . ? I'd rather die . . . yes,
die . . . that's better than this. DEATH IS THE FINAL SOLUTION OF
TAKING YOUR PAIN TO YOURSELF AND HUGGING IT TO DEATH . . .
DEATH IS YOUR PAIN TAKEN TO THE END . . . GET RID OF IT
SLOWLY . . . A BIT AT A TIME . . . How?! How?! I'm lonely and
miserable . . . How do you get rid of that? Eh! Tell me that!
ANALYSE IT . . . WHY AND HOW . . . AND THEN IT WILL
DISAPPEAR. Bollocks! It stays with me like a lump on my face or
a growth . . . in the morning when I get up, the night when I
sleep . . . my ache grows bigger and bigger . . . I'm starving for
friends and love I ache and hunger . . . SO WHAT DOES THE
STARVING MAN DO TO GET RID OF THE PAIN? Yeah . . . he
eats . . . where, show me where? Give me a clue, for God's
sake . . . I'll try anything . . . just show me . . . please God tell
me how? (*The phone rings . . . He is startled and rushes to the
phone; waits for it to ring a couple more times and picks it up.*)
Hallo . . . ? (*Trying to sound calm and relaxed*) Hallo? Who is
this? No, this is Harry. Yes! Oh, you have the wrong . . . no,
wait . . . who did you want? Terry? You don't mean Harry, do
you? No, definitely Terry. Wait . . . er, just a minute. Did he
live here? Oh, it's a different . . . no. That's OK . . . no, no
trouble . . . er sometimes it could sound the same . . .
Harry . . . Terry . . . yeah . . . er . . . what's your name . . . it
makes no difference . . . it's just that you sound like someone
I . . . sure, that's OK . . . have a nice Christmas . . . er, what
are you doing . . . (*Phone cuts off.*) Wrong number. Strange . . .
(*Stares at the phone a long time, picks it up and dials.*) No . . .
maybe she'll be in, it's late for Christmas . . . I'll meet her in a
pub . . . that's better than nothing . . . Hallo, is Clara there?
Harry . . . she's not . . . oh, out shopping . . . OK . . . no
message . . . oh wait, say that Harry called, will you . . . yeah,
Harry and to ring him . . . me . . . if she feels like a Christmas
drink . . . yeah, would you tell her that, please . . . sure, she
knows my number . . . bye . . . So that's OK . . . it makes it
easier if she doesn't ring . . . so that's it . . . yeah, that's
easier . . . she'll ring me if she wants to. That's good . . . feel

better. Analyse my pain . . . fah! I analyse a broken leg . . . it's
broken. BUT WHY? Oh shuddup! Shuddup! Shuddup! Shut the
voice up . . . it's broken because it's broken . . . there's no
why . . . it's done to you. NO, YOU DO IT TO YOURSELF. Jesus
Christ help me . . . SHIT SHIT SHIT SHIT.

Lights fade to black and then come up again.

Merry Christmas . . . no more cards . . . sod 'em . . . who
cares . . . do I shit and piss on the lot of you . . . (*Puts radio on:
carols, etc., maybe a sermon.*) It's only a day like any other . . .
across the length and breadth of Merry England the rosy faces
beam . . . greedy little fingers tear off the ribbons gazing in awe
at the wrong size shmutters they are forced to wear and granny
will sit in front of the flickering idiot box farting quietly away as
she dies slowly in a haze of chintz and lecithin chocolates.
Doorbells will ring and boring evil relatives will descend
grasping in their hands bottles of cheap plonk and more ghastly
toys for their stupid kids to scare the cat with. Nah! Who
cares . . . I didn't plan it right . . . Next year I'll arrange
something in advance . . . but not too far . . . maybe a couple of
weeks . . . just get myself together a bit more . . . yeah . . .
ring a few faces and not leave it to the last second . . . Clara
could have rung even if she couldn't see me . . . she might have
called . . . so what to do . . . listen to them all . . . shrieking
about nothing, sweating over their stupid turkey . . . still it
might have been nice to sit with a few faces and talk . . . I need
to talk . . . desperately . . . need to say a few things and tell
somebody something but their pain stays there like a lump and I
can't even do that . . . maybe that's why I am alone . . . maybe
I made it happen this way because I couldn't bear it . . . to sit
there and answer their stupid questions . . . "When you gonna
get hitched up Harry?" "What are you doing with yourself?"
"How's your life?" I have a nail through my head that gives me
a constant pain . . . could be through my hands . . . I feel
pinned . . . nailed up to my own cross . . . my own guilt . . . so
that's why I am alone . . . I have analysed it . . . my own guilt
for my own life. BUT WHERE DOES THE GUILT COME FROM? Who

cares? I was given a life and I didn't use it properly . . . I was
given a garden and I neglected it and I can't let anyone in the
gate because I am ashamed of how mouldy and overgrown the
garden is . . . weedy dishevelled dung heap . . . so that's the
answer . . . how it came to me! SO SUDDENLY LIKE A
REVELATION . . . HOW DID IT HAPPEN THIS GUILT? Happen? It
happened . . . I neglected the garden . . . I like that . . . I am a
garden of delights and there was one tree I cultivated until it was
bare and I ate off this one bloody tree but neglected all the rest
and the fruit of the tree yielded less and less fruit and smaller
and smaller because I didn't heed the rest or weed the garden
and so the roots became choked . . . oh shit, what am . . . what
am I saying . . . Ma . . . phone Ma . . . I can't sit there
again . . . watching the bleary eye that's wasting me away . . . I
can't . . . I'd rather sit here alone. (*Phones Ma.*) Ma! Happy
Christmas . . . yeah . . . listen, Ma . . . I'm a bit tied up . . .
yeah, people poppin' round . . . a party, etc . . . so I thought
I'd pop over for Boxing Day . . . are you sure . . . you'll be
OK? Sure? I can come if . . . no . . . no . . . I know I'm old
enough to please myself . . . but I don't want you to be lonely . . .
You're happy just to have a rest? Yeah, put your feet up and watch?
Oh good . . . yeah, you'll be OK . . . sure, I know, Ma . . . I love
you too . . . Haven't I said that before . . . 'course I have . . .
maybe it's because I know you know. I know you love me,
Ma . . . 'course I'll do what makes me happy . . . you're OK?
Good . . . yeah, tomorrow . . . see you then . . . yeah, the cat's
fine, he loved the pilchards . . . you have a nice Christmas too,
Ma, ta da . . . Maybe I'll sleep through the day . . . turn the
box on and nod off in front of Clark Gable. (*Goes to the box and
takes out some pills.*) One, two, three, no, maybe four, that's
enough. (*Swallows pills.*) Now I shall sit down and wait . . .
doesn't take too long . . . just have a nod and then it's all
over . . . Christmas is gone . . . housewives' pill, they call it.
How about a drop to wash it down with? (*Does so.*) Hey, that
felt pretty good . . . hey, I'm having a nice time here on my
lonesome . . . it ain't bad. WHAT'S NOT BAD – KILLING TIME
BECAUSE YOU CAN'T FACE YOURSELF . . . KILLING A BIT OF
YOURSELF SO AS NOT TO FEEL? I feel OK, so what . . . it is killing

a bit of yourself at a time . . . it's true . . . I'm burning up the
garden . . . or drowning it out . . . THE WEEDS WILL SURVIVE
AND CHOKE YOU UNLESS YOU TEAR THEM OUT . . . CLEAN IT
UP . . . START AGAIN. With what? Where do I start . . . go out in
the street . . . walk . . . run . . . do something . . . what?
Anything . . . get out of that room . . . don't just sit and
rot . . . don't look at that thing . . . it's a death-ray
machine . . . it pours evil rays into your head . . . maybe that's
what's wrong . . . I'll get out . . . where? I'll go to Clara's . . .
bust into their cosy Christmas dinner, say, "Here I am,
folks . . . Merry Christmas!" See their faces, what can they do,
chuck me out . . . No . . . they'll say, "Come in, Harry, what a
pleasant surprise . . . have a drink, old boy." I will. I'll say,
"Happy Christmas . . . I'm alone, you wouldn't want to enjoy
your turkey without me?" . . . do I dare, I wonder . . . it's better
than dying alone here . . . what's the worst that could
happen . . . they won't shoot me . . . I'll take a few more of
these things . . . it's beginning not to make any difference . . .
then I'll do it . . . Ha ha ha! WHAT AN ACHIEVEMENT . . . THE
SUM TOTAL OF YOUR COURAGE . . . TO KNOCK ON A DOOR. Yeah,
that's my achievement . . . to knock on a door . . . to build up
the courage to do what anyone in the world does normally I need
a mountain of courage to do . . . so what . . . who cares . . . I
must do something! I'll ring first, yes! I'll just ring and say,
"Clara, I'm coming over for a drink" . . . and she'll say, "Good,
Harry, just come over" . . . it's Christ's birthday for God's sake.
Didn't he die for us? Aren't we supposed on this day to give . . .
yeah . . . I'll just ring and say Merry Christmas and nothing
else . . . she'll say, "How are you spending it?" . . . and I'll say
"*Alone, you pig . . . alone and bleeding to death on the cross of my
own guilt*" and she'll say, "Come and have a sherry." (*Refers to
pills.*) The feeling isn't getting into me . . . (*Takes more pills.*)
One, two, three, four . . . five . . . six . . . more . . . it's too
much . . . but what the hell . . . how many is that? Ten or
twelve . . . oh well, it's Christmas . . . you can indulge . . . I'll
ring. (*Goes to the phone, picks it up . . . starts trembling, looks at it
and tries to dial, does so and clicks it off before it starts ringing, tries
it again and again; it clicks off.*) For Christ's sake, it's only a

call . . . wouldn't you be glad if someone called you? On
Christmas day . . . just say, "Have a nice Christmas, Clara" . . .
No! "Merry Christmas, Clara!" No. "Guess who this is,
Clara . . . hey . . . have a great Christmas . . . yeah, I'm taking it
easy . . . sure, I'll drop in . . . just for a few minutes!" Shit . . .
the pills're making me woozy. YOU'RE KILLING YOURSELF
SLOWLY INCH BY INCH SLOWLY BLEEDING TO DEATH. STOP IT . . .
STOP IT NOW . . . GO FOR A WALK . . . SEE THE SKY . . . VISIT
YOUR MOTHER . . . GO TO BED. SHOUT . . . SCREAM OR RUN . . .
GET OUT OF THIS ROOM. Get off the cross kid . . . but I like it
here . . . there's a good view . . . I'm above the crowd . . .
(*Takes more pills.*) One . . . two . . . three . . . four . . .
five . . . si–ix . . . No, that's enough . . . put me asleep for the
day then no more . . . awake tomorrow and see Mum . . .
Christmas over . . . I feel really good . . . hey, that's better . . .
no more pain . . . then that's what it's like . . . then it's
good . . . no more now . . . WHY NOT TAKE THE LOT AND BE RID
OF IT ALTOGETHER? THEN NO MORE CHRISTMAS . . . WHY GO
THROUGH THIS NEXT YEAR AND THE YEAR AFTER AND EACH DAY
AND EACH MINUTE . . . DON'T DIE IN BITS . . . DO IT NOW . . .
Then I'll ascend . . . THAT'S RIGHT . . . DON'T ANALYSE ANY
MORE . . . DON'T QUESTION THE PAIN . . . IT'S THERE . . .
YOU'RE RIGHT, YOU'RE BLEEDING TO DEATH SLOWLY . . . SO
HASTEN IT. Nah. Nah! that's defeatist . . . but I'll maybe just get
a taste . . . one . . . two . . . three . . . four . . . five . . .
six . . . and a couple more . . . (*Swallows.*) Be daring . . . go
on . . . don't stop at the edge . . . jump–Nah . . . I'm a
coward . . . NO, YOU'RE NOT . . . YOU'RE BRAVE NOW . . . IT'S
EASY AND IT'S PAINLESS WHEN YOU JUMP . . . YOU'LL SLEEP. Like
forever . . . it's tempting . . . Ha ha . . . Shit, it feels nice . . .
who will feed the cat? YOU LEAVE A NOTE . . . THE NEIGHBOURS
WON'T LET IT STARVE. I can't . . . what about Ma . . . she'll be
alone . . . she'll fret. SHE WON'T . . . SHE'LL UNDERSTAND . . .
YOU HAVE TO LIVE YOUR OWN LIFE . . . That's right . . .
OK . . . I feel good now . . . OK . . . I don't know how many
that is . . . maybe these will do . . . only ten left . . . OK . . .
I'm tired but the view is good . . . I can see the crowd running
about . . . but I'm still . . . and the wind is licking my face . . .

and the sun's warm . . . Clara's there! She's watching . . . and
smiling . . . she's proud . . . I loved Clara . . . Boy, this is some
trip . . . I see colours . . . Hey, Clara's taking me down . . . I
come off easily . . . like peeled off . . . and float down . . .
(*Drowsier and deeper as the drug takes effect*) We're together now
and walking along a beach! Come, Clara, let's have a run . . .
she tilts her head . . . her hair falls down like a waterfall . . .
she's smiling at me . . . what you giggling at . . . big blue
eyes . . . laughing . . . it's starting to rain we'll snuggle up in
the car . . . Hey, that's good . . . we're going to the
mountains . . . (*Miming*) we'll wrap up in the cold bedroom and
hold on tightly to each other . . . hold on tight, Harry, I'm
cold . . . sure . . . sure. There's no heat in this room . . . so
hang on . . . we're taking off . . . into the night . . . Ha! Ha!
Here we go . . . you asleep yet, Clara? No? We'll have breakfast
in bed . . . and . . . then . . . we'll have a walk . . . in the
mountains and be breathless and cold . . . we'll sing to keep
warm the songs we half remember . . . you start . . . shh . . .
go to sleep now . . . we've got a big day tomorrow . . . hold on
tight hold me . . . I fancy kippers and masses of toast and pints
of tea . . . do you mind if I have a smoke in bed . . . "I love
you, Harry" . . . "I love you too, Clara" . . . "How much?"
"Bucketsful" . . . it's really getting cold and the nights are
drawing in . . . (*The lights are fading and tightening, leaving only
his face.*) It's cold but we're OK . . . "Don't fall asleep with
your cigarette, Harry" . . . "I'll put it out . . . good night" . . .
we're floating into an endless night . . . we're going
upwards . . . taking off . . . hold on to me . . . always . . . hold
on . . . don't let go . . . you're slipping . . . away, Clara . . .
you have to hold on . . . don't go . . . don't . . . it's cold . . .
it's dark . . . where . . . are . . . you? I'm alone.

HARRY *is dead.*